WITCHCRAFT

Leanna Greenaway

Your Plain & Simple Guide to
Spells, Rituals, and Tools of Modern Wicca

HAMPTON ROADS

This edition first published in 2025 by Hampton Roads Publishing,
an imprint of Red Wheel/Weiser, LLC
With offices at:
65 Parker Street, Suite 7
Newburyport, MA 01950

Sign up for our newsletter and special offers by going to
www.redwheelweiser.com/newsletter

An earlier edition of this book was published as *Simply Wicca*
by Sterling Publishing Co., Inc. New York, © 2006 by Leanna Greenaway

The author and publisher are not responsible for any adverse effects or consequences resulting from the use of any practices, procedures, or preparations included herein. No responsibility is taken for the use of any herb, and although all of the herbs mentioned are understood to be safe, they should not be taken without consulting your medical professional.

Cover design by Sky Peck Design
Cover and interior art by SpicyTruffel/iStock
Interior design by Brittany Craig

ISBN: 978-1-64297-069-2

Library of Congress Cataloging-in-Publication Data available upon request

Printed in the United States of America
IBI
10 9 8 7 6 5 4 3 2 1

FSC MIX Paper FSC® C183721

DEDICATION

This book is dedicated to my wonderful husband, Graeme, who came into my life without any knowledge of Wicca and without ever having seen a tarot card. He patiently accepted my witchy way of life and even went on to cast the odd spell himself. He has created my altar, designed my pentagrams, and even polished my wand. Through all of the ups and downs, his support and devotion extended further, to my precious children, who now call him Dad. Taking on a ready-made family, when you have no children of your own, is no easy task, but what a brilliant job he has done so far.

Contents

Foreword

While writing my book, *Encyclopedia of Witchcraft*, one of my research methods was to simply insert the word "witch" into every possible search engine I could find, just to see what emerged. I did this with standard search engines, like Google, but also with literally any website that allowed me to search, from eBay to book sellers to museum databases. Using this technique, I discovered all sorts of things about witches and witchcraft that I might not otherwise have learned: some of these things were fun or charming, some were surprising or insightful, and, inevitably, because of the topic, some were tragic.

During one of these searches, I came across an extremely poignant website that had been created to serve as a testimonial and memorial to a Colonial American woman who had been falsely and cynically accused of practicing witchcraft. Like so many others in this situation, she had been convicted and executed. The website was beautifully written by this woman's descendant and I was very moved by it. Her story described how the ancestor had run afoul of a powerful man and the fatal results. This was relevant to my research, as my *Encyclopedia of Witchcraft* contains an extensive section on the history of witch-hunting. Because this particular website was so deeply personal and touching, I wished to include its link in my own book, so that other readers could experience it, just as I had.

I emailed the site, politely explaining my book project and offering the link to my website, so that she could see my previous publications and that this was a genuine request. Nothing on the site warned me of the response I would receive.

Trial of Martha Corey, illustration by John W. Ehninger, in "Giles Corey of the Salem Farms" (1868).

That response was *immediate*. In no uncertain terms, the author expressed her strong desire *not* to be quoted in my book. She did not want her link included and, furthermore, demanded that the story of her ancestor *not* be included in the book at all. In her own words, she told me that she did not want her beloved ancestor "associated with those awful people"—and by awful people, she meant witches, not their executioners or accusers. Perhaps she meant me.

This occurred in approximately 2005. It was the age of the internet, not sometime way back in the medieval era or during the dark ages or before the social revolutions of the 1960s. Even today, as I write, although we are in the midst of a metaphysical renaissance, witches still evoke mixed reactions. For every individual like me, who loves and adores witches, who perceives them as heroes, there are others who consider them to be awful . . . or worse.

Now, you may argue, many of those who perceive witches in a negative light are simply ignorant; they don't understand the witch's true identity. Blinded and deceived by old prejudices and stereotypes, they can't see the inherent beauty of witchcraft: its pride in female empowerment; the way it encourages people to mingle with angels, animal and plant spirits, and the benevolent powers of the universe; and, most especially, the manner in which witchcraft encourages human efforts to harmonize with the elements, the Sun, the tides, Mother Earth, and especially the Moon; to find our own unique place and power within the cosmos.

There are those who blame this inability to see on etymology. They claim that the word "witch" itself, with its centuries of negative usage, has become irrevocably tainted. According to this school of thought, if only we could consciously create new ways of expression, then a clear, neutral view of witchcraft might become possible and prejudice would end.

Of course, "witch" is not the only word to be considered in this fashion. Back when I was a teenager in the 1970s, many words were closely analyzed and reinterpreted. Words, an integral part of the spell-casting process, possess the power to define and to redefine, to guide or control how something is perceived and understood. Thus, during this era, names of ethnic groups, for instance, were consciously tweaked and adjusted. Similarly, during this time, some began to use the word "wiccan" as a synonym for "witch." Witchcraft is a sprawling topic that defies efforts to contain and classify it and so perhaps it's natural that rather than producing clarity, this effort only increased the already-existing confusion.

The word "witch" may refer to someone of any gender who practices the magical arts. It may refer to a beautiful and thus "bewitching" woman. Yet some use that same word to shame old women or to brand a woman as difficult or unpleasant. Historically, "witch" has been used to describe midwives and practitioners of herbal medicine. Nowadays, it may also refer to adherents of Wicca, the Earth-centered religion that celebrates the Wheel of the Year. If someone asks *you* if you're a witch, it's best to know what they mean by that word before you answer.

Language evolves with time. Beginning in the 1970s, many understood "wiccan" to be a kinder, gentler, more respectful word for "witch." Now, in the 21st century, "wiccan" more typically refers to practitioners of the religion known as Gardnerian Wicca. Yet the influence of the '70s still lingers and many use the words interchangeably, as does Leanna Greenaway in this book.

In *Witchcraft,* Greenaway has crafted a contemporary approach to Wicca and witchcraft. Among the many beauties of witchcraft is the freedom of spiritual expression that it offers. Magical practice hones our senses, our ability to see and to hear with enhanced clarity and perception, to transcend the simple boundaries of language. May this book assist you on your own personal path and bring you joy.

—Judika Illes, author of
Pure Magic and other books of magic

Preface

Wicca is personal to many of those who follow it, and witches have many faces. There are Traditional Witches, who form sociable pagan religious covens, and while this book may interest that group, it is not particularly written for them. I have sought to demonstrate modern Wicca, which is suitable for any person to follow, on her own or as part of a like-minded family or group. One of the beauties of Wicca, or witchcraft, is that it is nonjudgmental. It doesn't enforce a list of stringent rules that one has to follow in order to gain acceptance. It is even possible for someone to belong to one of the formal religions, or any other type of spiritual discipline, and still follow some form of Wicca. The only belief that we all have, whether we are Traditional Witches, Hedge Witches, or any other kind of witch, is that we never seek to harm or maliciously influence others.

It is noticeable among today's young adults—the so-called "millennials"—that there is a keen desire to preserve and respect our planet and its animal life. There is a greater trend in growing and eating organic food without necessarily becoming fanatical about it, or even taking up vegetarianism. There is a genuine interest in personal self-development, and understanding how spirituality, religious belief, social and global consciousness all relate to our place in the universe. Modern Wicca fits very well with this warm and caring modern ideal. So, whether or not you take up some or all of the Wiccan beliefs discussed in this book, I wish you all the very best of luck. Let us allow everyone to follow their true path and hinder no one!

Contrary to belief, not all witches are female; there are male and female witches in every town and village in the world. I need to point out that I have specifically used the feminine gender in this book. I have done this because women are the principal readers of this kind of material, and anyway, it makes a change from the norm.

Disclaimer

This book is designed to educate and entertain while providing information regarding the subject matter covered. It is sold with the understanding that the publishers and author are not thereby engaged in rendering legal, medical, or any other professional services. If such services are required, the services of a competent professional should be sought. The author and the publisher shall have neither liability nor responsibility to any person or entity with respect to any loss or damage caused, or alleged to have been caused, directly or indirectly by the information contained in this book.

Every effort has been made to make this book as complete and as accurate as possible while still maintaining its plain and simple approach. However, there may be mistakes, both typographical and in content; this book comes from my experience of Wicca at this point in time. Therefore, the text should be used only as a general guide and not as the ultimate source of information on the subjects covered. Those interested in following the Wiccan path are encourage to delve into the many excellent books available for further study.

—Leanna Greenaway

CHAPTER ONE

Witches and Magic

Magic dates back to the beginning of everything; to a time when human beings relied upon instinct and were fully in tune with the elements. Over the centuries, religions evolved throughout the world to include a belief in myth, mysteries, ritual, and the supernatural as part of their mystique.

Why did our ancestors need magic? Even today people worship Mother Nature, and many are reviving the old ways and traditions and adapting them to our modern way of life. So do we need magic today? To answer this question, we must first look at the history of humankind and how we have progressed throughout our time on this planet.

The Bronze Age blacksmith was acknowledged within his community as a priest or superior spiritual figure. To his fellow villagers, it appeared that he sat on the outskirts of his village and magically conjured blades, weapons, and stunning jewelry from stones. To a person living in the Bronze Age, this was nothing short of a miracle. We all know that we can make bronze by heating a combination of copper and tin to a very high temperature, but to the people of that time, these skills were considered to be miraculous and so, of course, the blacksmith was revered.

In the past there were "wise women" who were renowned for their skills in healing the sick; they used their knowledge of plants and herbs to cure certain ailments. Nowadays we would call them midwives, nurses, or doctors. It was only in the 16th century, when the witch hunts began, that these people and their knowledge were forced underground.

Magic and sorcery were common practices in many cultures, such as the Egyptian, Native American, and among the shamans of Central and South America. With each civilization, the method of ritual varied, but the principles were the same. Chanting and spell casting were used with the understanding that they would attract favor from the gods, who would grant good fortune.

Now, in the 21st century, we have become more advanced. Most of us are well informed and educated and live happily alongside science and technology. Today, almost everyone in the developed world has a mobile phone or smartphone and a computer. We can communicate with people in different countries with just a touch of a button, or we can climb inside a huge piece of metal and fly across the sky. We can flick a switch and drive out the night with electric lighting. Our ancestors would surely think us magicians! It is quite possible that, in a similar fashion, what seems magical to us may turn out to be quite natural in the future. Magic has always had its place in the world, and it probably always will.

The power of prayer has been recognized for many centuries; therefore, the spiritual world cannot be overlooked. I am a believer, but I am also extremely grounded. Because I've been a witch for the greater part of my life, I often use magic to change the energies around me and to bring about a more positive vibration. Ritual can also change a person's frame of mind, bringing confidence where there is none and lending a sense of proportion to difficult situations. With this in mind, magic should not be thrown out in favor of all that is mechanical or scientific just because many people don't understand it; magic brings us spiritual benefits that we should not ignore.

Karma and reincarnation are core beliefs in the Wiccan faith, and one of our tenets is "As you sow, so shall you reap." In accordance with this belief, we are careful not to incur bad karma by hurting anyone, either emotionally or physically. A modern witch will always endeavor to do the right thing and to protect and nurture everything around her, however big or small. Let's face it: Our planet is awesome and nature can be overwhelming, so much so that there has to be a greater source that has created something this beautiful and complex. I still have many unanswered questions, but as a child I was taught by my mamma that if something feels right to you in your heart, then you should believe it. If it doesn't, then you should leave it alone.

It is important always to recognize your inner truth, because it will seldom let you down. This is why witchcraft has struck a chord within me. It's about recognizing the balance and harmony of the planet and our relationship to it. Once you come to grips with that belief, you can comprehend so much more than you otherwise could about the spiritual side of life.

Another reason that I love Wicca is that there are no specific rules. Personally, I don't like rigidity and I prefer to express myself spiritually, without a rule book in my hand. I have never been one to follow and absorb old philosophies blindly, and I feel sorry for certain individuals who are too stubborn to move on and who are stuck in a rut in this life, and no doubt were in past lives, too.

Wicca is an individual faith that you can adjust and tweak to suit yourself. Of course, there are traditional teachings that you can follow if you want to, but religion has to move with the times. By virtue of your free will, you can bring your faith up to date. For instance, a few years ago I inadvertently cast a spell on top of the microwave while I was defrosting some meat. I was at one of my lazy stages in life, when I didn't have the time to set up an altar. To my surprise, the spell didn't take the usual week or so to work; the results were almost immediate. I got to thinking that maybe magic works well with electricity, and after casting several other spells on top of the microwave, I found that the theory proved to be right! I've since tried my ritual techniques on top of the television, beside the computer, and next to the radio. They all worked!

With Wicca, there is no right way or wrong way. There are no rigid commandments to follow, and you don't have to attend meetings, or go to church, or divulge all in the confessional box. You don't even have to share your beliefs with anyone else if you don't want to. You can join a gathering known as a coven, or you can be a Solitary Witch—it's a purely personal decision. Wicca is a private way of life that you can adapt and fit to any busy schedule. This flexibility is useful, because if you do decide to study the traditional methods, you can eliminate the parts you don't particularly connect with and adapt the ideas to your own way of thinking.

Let's now quash the common fear associated with the word "witchcraft."

Witchcraft stems from paganism, which is the oldest known religion. The name comes from the title "wise craft" or "the way of the wise." A more recent term is "Wicca craft" (the word "Wicca" being linked with the wick of a candle). After centuries of hype, people still shy away from the word "witch," thinking that some evil woman with a big black hat and a warty nose is out to turn them into a frog or worse! It is simply not the case. Today's witch would not hurt a fly. Sixteenth-century prejudice created the misconception that any form of magic or spell making was wicked and evil. Pagan folk, who worshiped a lovable goat-like being called Pan, were denounced as devil worshippers and banished to the hills in fear for their lives. Pan was thus corrupted to become Satan or the devil, but not by witches.

Nowadays, the freedom and better education of the modern age mean that witches from all walks of life are able to come out of the closet. The old ways have slipped back into their rightful place, and we are at last free to pray and worship in the style in which we feel comfortable. So the next time you meet someone who claims to be a witch, tip your hat and think, "Now, there's a wise woman!"

General Wiccan Belief

A person who follows the essence of Wicca respects the Earth and seeks to live in harmony with nature. Witches don't intend to harm or offend any creature or individual in our path. We just adore living things, gardens, and any form of horticulture. Growing things gladdens the heart, while the onset of a new life—such as a germinating seed—brings contentment and fulfillment.

It is known that the Moon and Sun affect the energies surrounding the Earth and that they also influence situations and the nature of humankind. People following the Wiccan way assign great importance to lunar cycles and conduct their rituals according to the current Moon phase.

We can attune ourselves and tap into our psyches to achieve results for the good of others. Wiccans like to practice healing

techniques such as reiki, psychic projection, and clairvoyance. We have an interest in anything supernatural or unexplained and we lean toward alternative therapies such as hypnosis, acupuncture, and homeopathy. We also promote self-awareness through meditation and visualization. We accept the paranormal and we look into spiritual issues for solutions to problems.

For us, the Earth is a place of learning, a bit like a school. We reincarnate on Earth and live as long as our destiny permits. During this time, we must try to address and empathize with every situation we face. By a successful completion of this process, we hope to further our spiritual development. When our time has come to leave this world, we return to the astral plane, known in other faiths as Nirvana, Heaven, or Paradise. If we choose, we can reincarnate again, in the hope of fulfilling and accomplishing the things that we couldn't manage in our previous incarnation.

To us, all that is living is equal. We are no better than the insects, plants, and animals with which we coexist. However,

Wiccans do appreciate and respect that there have to be certain people who establish laws and rules for our own well-being and for the good of society.

Witches don't worship or believe in Satan or the devil, as defined by the Christian tradition. We believe that the devil is a Christian concept that was used many centuries ago to intimidate and frighten people in order to convert from other faiths. Ill will toward another being is not tolerated in Wicca, nor do we desire the power to control others.

Wicca is so widespread that there is no right or wrong way to follow the faith. Certain individuals have a preference for selected areas of the craft, and these folk concentrate more on particular aspects of Wicca. For instance, you may find that one witch will be more interested in spell casting quietly at home, whereas another will follow a more traditional approach and work outdoors in a coven. Whichever sort of witch you choose to be is a personal decision for you. Below are just a few of the preferences.

The Traditional Witch

Although I speak of witches as female, both men and women can practice witchcraft, and both are referred to as witches.

The Traditional Witch believes very much in the "old ways" and will worship her relevant gods and goddesses. Her belief is conventionally pagan and she will celebrate the pagan Sabbats.

The Gardnerian Tradition

The Gardnerian tradition was founded by Gerald Gardner and promulgated in the 1950s; he brought witchcraft back into the limelight and created a tremendous amount of media interest. His main aim was to reintroduce the craft after hundreds of years of dormancy. The main spur to this openness was the repeal of the Witchcraft Act in Britain in 1951.

The Hereditary Witch

Wicca tends to run in families, so the Hereditary Witch can trace her roots back to distant relatives. She may have been taught and guided by family members.

The Hedge Witch

The Hedge Witch believes that all living things have a spirit. Just as the human being has a soul, so the animals, plants, trees, and vegetables also have their own spirits. It may sound ludicrous to some that a potato has a spirit, but the spirit is a type of vibration. It is scientific fact that all matter has its own vibration.

We know that crystals are created from the Earth's elements. Amber's origin is fossilized resin; many other stones, such as emeralds, are formed by hydrothermal veins, which are caused by

hydrothermal fluids breaking away from the hot magma, deep in the Earth's crust. The Hedge Witch is extremely tuned in to the living elements and believes in the power of gemstones and crystals. Hedge Witches don't believe in Satan, but they do accept that there is a substantial amount of negativity in this world, so they strive to dispel any negative vibrations through dowsing and cleansing procedures. Like the Kitchen Witch, Hedge Witches grow most of their own produce and prepare potions for the best intent. Hedge Witches have a devout belief in reincarnation, and they believe that when people die, they are taken to the spirit world, where they are healed and are made ready to be born again.

The term "Hedge Witch" describes a person who doesn't belong to a coven or a tradition, but who works alone. She is usually self-taught. She will rarely go through a formal initiation, but she will enjoy mixing with other like-minded people. In any event, she tends to keep her findings, such as recipes, potions, and spells, to herself.

The Kitchen Witch

The Kitchen Witch is similar to the Hedge Witch in her practices. She believes in the importance of all living things, but she is a bit more hands-on in her approach. A Kitchen Witch makes most of her own personal products, such as soaps, shampoos, and moisturizers. She may even go as far as making her own candles and incense. In her view, everything has to be pure and sterile, so by creating her tools from scratch, she eliminates negative influences that can innocently be transmitted through store-bought goods. Interestingly, many candles are made in sweatshops, and the people employed are often under-paid, unhappy, bored, and maybe even mistreated, so there can be a negative energy in the candles. The Kitchen Witch would not tolerate this, as her spells and candles have to be of the very highest vibration so that she can get the best results from them.

If you see yourself as a Kitchen Witch, then you will endeavor to be eco-friendly and to grow your own herbs for spells, oils, potions, and the food that you eat.

The Solitary Witch

Solitary Witches don't belong to a coven, and they tend to keep their faith strictly secret. These witches prefer to remain anonymous. Like the Hedge and Kitchen Witches, they celebrate the seasons and the Sabbats, and they mix their own blends of potions and spells to help those around them. They don't tend to be as fanatical organically as Hedge and Kitchen Witches, but they like the outdoors and have an appreciation for scenery. Because there is far less prejudice against witches today, solitary practitioners are sometimes happy to be open about their faith, but they generally go about their business peacefully and keep to themselves. One of the lovely things about these witches is that they aren't eccentric and they keep their feet on the ground.

Covens

History has it that in ancient times, when witches were persecuted, many pagans took to the hills to worship their gods and goddesses in secret. These groups became known as covens. Nowadays, a coven consists of a group of individuals who share a common interest. Some Wiccans long to be part of a like-minded group with whom they can share spells and wisdom. Finding a coven to suit you isn't easy, as the organizers tend not to advertise them. Many people over the years have asked me how they can join a group, but I cannot give them an answer because these covens are very close-knit and anonymous. Much is learned only through word of mouth over a period of time, so an element of luck is involved in the process.

A while ago I decided to run a cyber-coven, which has become very successful. Unfortunately, with members from all over the world, setting up meetings can be tricky. In the hope of overcoming this problem, we invested in a good chat-room and message-board facility, thus enabling the members to communicate freely with one another. We can still perform rituals together online, and those who are at different stages of development can be taught and guided by the more experienced among us. Maybe this is the new way forward for all high-tech witches!

Angelic Wicca

The god and goddess have always been connected to witchcraft in one way or another, and although many witches still prefer this way of practice, there is now a new vibration called Angelic Wicca. Angels are becoming more popular, and many witches, like me, prefer to work with this newfound angel energy.

Many Wiccans are gravitating to this way of thinking because the god and goddess theory is now a little out of touch. The people

I speak to are more comfortable with angelic worship and find it far more personal. Just as members of other religions pray, so do witches. We all light candles and perform our rituals, but whatever your faith, angels are eagerly accepted, and no one feels threatened or intimidated at the thought of them. This is why my fellow coven witches and I have chosen to follow the Angelic Wiccan path.

CHAPTER TWO

Wicca and Positive Thought

All of us at some time or other have wished that we could wave a magic wand and make everything better. Well, to a certain extent we can. A little gentle magic every now and then can change your life, but there are times when no amount of spell casting or magical intervention will help. From a karmic point of view, there are some situations that we are not allowed to control, and if our fate requires us to stand still for a while, then we have to wait until it is our time to move ahead. Each person we meet, each problem we face, helps us to grow spiritually in one way or another. A favorite expression of mine is that life is like a big classroom. With each day, we learn and encounter new experiences, and although at times the problems we face are hard, by going through these processes, we climb that spiritual ladder and evolve to a higher plane. I look back sometimes on how difficult my life has been, but the hard times have brought wisdom and knowledge that I wouldn't trade for the world.

In most cases, however, we *are* in control of our lives, and for those situations that we *can* change, it is absolutely vital that magic is used positively and that rituals are conducted with good intent. Always make sure you are in the right frame of mind before you begin spell casting. If you are feeling ill, angry, or emotional in any way, your spell may be thwarted, so you should wait until you have settled down. Magic is about creating a harmonious setting and leaving the energies around you uncontaminated. A negative frame of mind will quickly turn an innocent spell into something much darker—and the negative thoughts you have projected will do a U-turn and bounce back in your direction. A thought is a living thing and it carries power. Just as we can physically strike others, we can also mentally attack them by building up a stream of emotional, disruptive aggression, with similar results.

Wiccan Ground Rules

These are some of the beliefs that many witches and pagans regard as their basic ground rules.

- Witches worship the earth around us. We seek to live in harmony with nature and to do no intentional injustice to any creature or person in our path.
- The Moon is important to witches. We believe that it affects the energies surrounding the planet and controls the situations and the moods of mankind.
- We believe in both an outer world and an inner world, which we call our spirit world.
- We believe that the earth is a place of learning. We come here for a short time and learn life's lessons to further our spiritual development.
- We believe that we are all equal, but we appreciate and respect that there must be certain people who set out laws and rules for our own well-being.
- We do not advocate ill will toward another being nor do we delight in power or influence over others. We work only for the good and well-being of other individuals.

CHAPTER THREE

Tools for the Beginner Witch

Various types of tools and objects are used to perform spells. Some are used as symbolic representations, while others, such as candles and incense, are more practical. The tools differ from spell to spell, but whichever collection you decide to use, your personal choice is paramount. Many people are discouraged because some ingredients or tools are hard to obtain, but remember that a certain amount of flexibility is possible, and improvisation is fine. That said, there are a few mandatory things you will need to take on board.

The Altar

You will need a base to work from, and the magical term for this base is the "altar." When you begin to create your altar, it's important that you make it your own, completely personal to you. Each witch will design her altar differently; this is because there are no set rules that say that an altar must be created a certain way.

Not everyone's home has adequate space to house a full-size altar, and some witches would rather not broadcast their beliefs by having a large display. A table top or shelf works perfectly well, as does a coffee table or a mantelpiece. If you love fabric and wish to have your altar covered in a cloth, you can buy or make an inexpensive cover. Some witches prefer to spell cast upon natural wood, in which case a cloth isn't necessary. If you're an "out of the closet" witch, you could leave your altar set out all the time, so that it is easily accessible when you need to conduct a ritual. For those who want to be more discreet or who don't have the space, a portable altar can be easily fashioned by placing a cloth on a hard floor and laying out the tools on top. This method is also handy if you are traveling.

The Pentagram

The pentagram dates back to around 3500 BCE, and it has always been associated with myth and magic. Since ancient times, this symbol has been known to protect the owner, and the pentagram was frequently worn as an amulet to celebrate spiritual protection and a happy homecoming. Should the pentagram be turned upside down, the image then becomes the pagans' god Pan, the horned god. Sadly with Christianity, the pentagram became equated with the devil and no longer held its true meaning. Lots of Wiccans wear the five-pointed star around their necks in jewelry form and use it as a way of recognizing fellow witches. The five points of the star represent protection and symbolize the five elements, earth, air, fire, water, and spirit, starting with the top point as earth, then traveling clockwise around the star.

Today we are lucky enough to have the internet, and objects such as pentagrams are now readily available. For the ultimate protection when spell casting, it is good to have a pentagram placed on your altar. The size isn't terribly important, but its position is. Usually the best place to situate your pentagram is directly in the center of your altar, with the star facing you in the upright position.

Once you have acquired your pentagram, you will need to charge it. This is a simple but necessary procedure if you want the best results from your spells. Some like to leave the pentagram in the garden overnight during a full Moon phase, so that the power of the Moon can cleanse and charge it naturally. I personally love this approach and charge everything magical in this way. Tools and objects, such as crystals and talismans, will absorb the power from the Moon and Earth. Once in the garden, you must close your eyes and meditate for about five minutes, trying to clear your mind. Imagine that you have an invisible eye in the center of your forehead (known as the inner eye or third eye.) Next, you must picture a bright purple light radiating from your inner eye and pointing directly to the pentagram. In the morning, your pentagram will be fully charged; its power should last for about a month. If you live in an apartment and do not have access to a garden, you can place the pentagram in a bowl of salt water and leave it overnight.

Salt and Water

It is imperative that you have salt and water on your altar. Being entirely natural substances, they offer the highest forms of protection. Place a small bowl of salt and another one of water on either side of the pentagram.

Candles

All good witches have an endless supply of candles in their home, and because some spells require specific colors, most modern witches opt for the tea-light version, as they come in every color, they are inexpensive, and they burn down quickly. Purchase a selection; if you are ever unsure of which color to use, use a white one. The following list will give you a good idea of which candle colors represent particular situations.

- White: Any situation
- Black: Prevention from psychic attack
- Blue: House moving and property matters
- Red: Passion
- Pink: Love
- Green: Money and wealth
- Yellow, orange, or gold: Health
- Purple: Protection and employment

Incense

It is said that for a spell to work properly, the environment has to be right. So you need to create a certain ambience for effective spell casting. By burning incense for the duration of a spell, you are setting the scene for positive spell casting.

I use the sandalwood type of incense for most of my rituals, as it is renowned for clearing away negative energies.

The Chalice

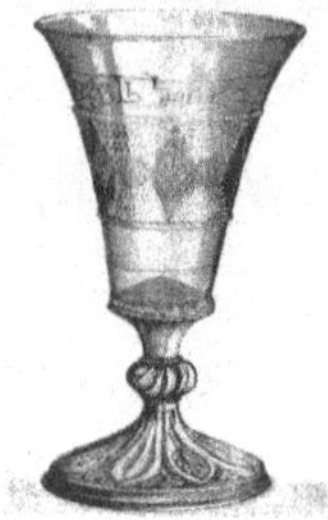

The chalice represents the element of water. It is a symbol of fertility, and in ancient times it often corresponded to the womb of the goddess. The stand is symbolic of the material world, the stem represents the relationship between humanity and spirit, and the lip or rim of the chalice is thought to attract spiritual force.

The Cauldron

The cauldron is probably the tool most commonly associated with witchcraft, and it is drenched in magical tradition. Today, the cauldron is used as a vessel for making infusions and potions. Some spells involve burning herbs and other such items, and the cauldron is a good device to use, as most are made from copper or cast iron. Be aware that cauldrons can be hard to find, so you will need to persevere if you want one.

The Bell

The bell is a ritual tool used in banishment spells. It can be rung either to indicate the start of a spell, enabling the clearing of any negativity, or repeatedly around the home to get rid of unwanted vibrations. Bells can also be used to safeguard the home by dispelling evil spirits, or to stir up good energies.

The Athame

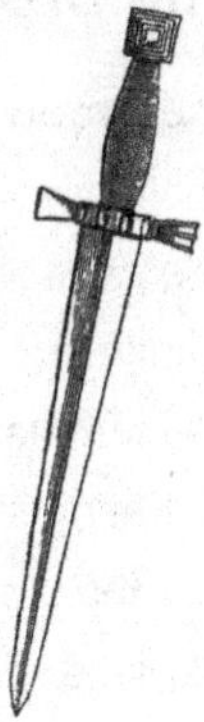

The athame (pronounced *a-thah-may*) is the conventional ritual knife. The traditional dagger usually has a black handle with a double-edged blade. Many witches inscribe their candles with an athame and cast a magical circle around the altar before commencing rituals. The athame is thought to work by transporting power from us through it. It is used only for magical purposes, so the blades are normally not sharpened.

The Wand

The wand is one of the primary magical tools. Traditionally, it is made from the wood of the willow, elder, apple, or cherry tree. The length of your wand should measure from your elbow to the tip of your index finger. These days you can easily purchase wands, but the maker of the wand channels the real magical power into it, so it is much better to make your own. If you decide to do this, you must always thank the tree from which your wand came. You can carve the wand or sand it down, then varnish it and charge it. The wand is a summoning tool that is used to evoke the spirits. It is also used to bless and charge objects and to draw down the Moon during spell casting.

The Broomstick

The broomstick, or besom, as it is more traditionally known, is a phallic symbol, and female witches used to use it in fertility rites. The sweeping end corresponds to the female genitals and the staff is linked with the male, making the entire tool a symbol of the male and female together.

Besoms were often placed near the hearth of the home to protect the opening, and many Wiccans still believe a besom at the fireplace will prevent evil from entering there. By sweeping the dust from the home, you are symbolically casting out bad energy. At a hand-fasting (a witch's wedding), couples jump onto the broom to display their union. Have you ever heard the old expression "living over the brush"? This was said when a couple lived together without having formally tied the knot.

Crystals and Gemstones

I feel great affection for crystals and, as they have a purely natural magic all their own, I place at least three on my altar at all times. Turquoise is great for protection spells, and amethyst and citrine work brilliantly for healing rituals, while clear quartz and rose quartz add to the power of a spell by cleansing the area. It is worth buying a good book on crystals and their meanings to get an idea about which ones are best to use for the task at hand.

The Book of Shadows

The Book of Shadows is a workbook in which a witch records her spells and rituals. All spells the witch casts are noted down for future reference. It also works as a dream diary, and it contains a Moon phase calendar that can easily be detached and replaced each year. Usually the Book of Shadows is handwritten, but today many witches prefer to use a computer and keep the information safely backed up.

CHAPTER FOUR

Lunar Magic

The Moon has always been known to exert a magical influence on the Earth. Scientists are always adding to their knowledge of the Moon's activities and are bringing more understanding to the way it affects our planet. It is interesting to note that many scientists studying the Moon have become more in touch with their spiritual side, while those fortunate enough to travel into space have often returned in a more spiritual frame of mind.

The Moon is traditionally linked with the feminine aspect and the functions of the right side of the brain, which tend to influence creativity and insight. Men also possess these functions, but they tend to be found more abundantly in women.

The Moon sits approximately 250,000 miles away from the Earth. We generally say the Moon takes 28 days to complete its orbit around the Earth, but in reality it is 29.5 days—this latter time is longer due to the movement of the Earth during the Moon's orbit.

There are many theories about the Moon and how it affects us. One theory posits that the Moon and its phases influence our internal chemistry, pulling on the gravitational forces of our physical bodies. Another concept states the gravitational field of a full Moon changes energy particles that reach the Earth, influencing the way we think and feel by changing the functions of our brain.

The word "lunatic" came into use because people suffering mental imbalances tended to become unstable at the time of a full Moon. Of course, the human body is about 80 percent water, so as the Moon affects the tides, perhaps it also changes the tide of our lives!

Dating as far back as humanity's earliest tribes, the Sun, the Moon, and the stars were identified as having control over women and pregnancy. When we look at the connections between women and the Moon, we see that the female menstrual cycle lasts roughly 29.5 days. This is the length of time between two full Moons. Another interesting thing to note is that a pregnancy is around 266 days long, which is the approximate number of days within ten full Moons. It's uncanny how women, especially in their fertile years, may be affected by the lunar cycle.

A very interesting experiment that you may wish to try is to study your own mood changes throughout the month and to note down how you feel during each Moon phase. You may be quite surprised at the results. My friend Sasha suggests that you also check how you, your family, and your friends or colleagues behave when the Moon passes through different signs of the zodiac. For instance, many people become irritable, angry, and subjective when the Moon is in a fire sign (Aries, Leo, or Sagittarius), or they may overwork when it is in an earth sign (Taurus, Virgo, or Capricorn). They may be somewhat unemotional and more detached and objective than usual when the Moon is in an air sign (Gemini, Libra, or Aquarius) and more intuitive and instinctive when it is in a water sign (Cancer, Scorpio, or Pisces).

The Full Moon

Research shows that when the Moon is full, more traffic accidents, murders, and suicides take place than at any other time during the lunar cycle. Those unfortunate enough to endure mental or emotional problems can experience difficulties around this phase. It has also been documented that people with criminal tendencies tend to offend more around this time.

From a magical point of view, a full Moon is an excellent time to cast love spells, as the power from the full Moon intensifies emotional matters.

Cast spells during the full Moon for:

- Marriage
- Romance
- Harmony in relationships
- Beauty
- Musical talents
- Psychic abilities

The Waxing Moon

When the Moon is waxing (growing into a full Moon), many witches cast spells to remove blocks and to improve life in general. Rituals can be performed if you feel that you are in a rut and if circumstances around you are not changing quickly enough. The energies at this time tend to work in a very positive fashion and usually bring about the desired results quite quickly.

Cast spells during a waxing Moon for:

- Problems at work
- Health
- Money

- Education
- Self-discipline
- Moving house or property matters

The Waning Moon

Magically, the waning Moon (when the Moon is shrinking toward a new Moon) is a good time to cast spells to remove unwanted situations and to shift negative or bad influences. There are times when we may feel like we don't have the strength to tackle certain individuals, or that we lack the confidence that we need to face up to our fears. Spell casting during this phase gives us the power to take control, strengthen our inner selves, and become more assertive in our actions. It can also help us to find something that we have mislaid.

Cast spells during a waning Moon for:

- Banishing enemies
- Clearing negative vibrations
- Harassment
- Confidence
- Courage
- Willpower
- Being bullied

- Assertiveness
- Emotional healing
- Lost property

The New Moon

Spells cast during a new Moon can bring many new changes: buying a new home, starting a new job, enjoying a blossoming relationship. White Witches favor the new Moon phase when spell casting to bring about new beginnings of some kind. Usually, a spell to be rid of a problem or unwelcome situation would commence on a waning Moon; the witch would then wait until the new Moon to bring about the positive replacement.

Cast spells during a new Moon for

- Conception
- New jobs
- New relationships
- Weddings
- Travel
- Money matters
- Parenting
- Communication
- Legal matters

The Dark of the Moon

Casting spells during the dark of the Moon should be done after you are no longer a beginner on the Wiccan path. I mention this Moon phase here because it should be included in a plain and simple introduction to Wicca. The dark of the Moon takes place shortly before a new Moon. It's a brief phase, and during this time the Moon appears invisible—some people confuse the dark Moon with the new Moon.

Spells cast during a dark Moon are especially potent because this Moon phase seems to give a "boost" to spell working. Witches find this a good time to tackle personal issues that are destructive in life—addictions, anger, serious disease. But because this is such a potent time for spell casting, workings that are meant to be "destructive"—that is, destroying unwanted negativity—in the hands of a beginner can become spells that are "harmful"—that is, casting negativity and harm onto others. Wicca is a pure and natural faith that aims to harm no one. If you are an inexperienced witch, a ritual or spell cast at this time could have an opposite effect and bring about an unwanted situation.

I recommend using the strength of this Moon phase for meditation and soul-searching, not for ritual work.

☽ ☽ ☽

Many modern calendars list the dates and phases of the Moon, so it is a good idea to purchase one each year to find out exactly what the Moon is doing. This way you are sure to work your magic on the correct days.

CHAPTER FIVE

Initiation

Initiation is one of those words that always has a whiff of "exclusive club" about it. This is not the case at all. The process of initiation simply means that you are dedicating yourself to something, making your commitment official. Initiation into Wicca means that you have found a home in the practice, and you want to acknowledge and honor that.

There is a difference between initiation into the craft and initiation into a coven. Initiation into the craft should always be a private ritual, a solitary moment between you and your angel or divine source. The procedure is simple and allows you to accept the faith wholeheartedly and to follow its basic guidelines. A coven initiation involves a member of the group, usually the high priest or priestess, conducting a ceremony that welcomes an individual into the family of witches.

If you like the idea of practicing magic, it is a good idea to initiate yourself; the process is just like conducting a spell, only this time you are focusing solely on yourself. It is vital to have the correct tools and settings, though, so follow the instructions in the next sections carefully.

Self-Dedication and Initiation

Step 1

The Moon needs to be in positive phase; a new Moon or, even better, a full Moon phase is the best time to perform the ritual. Avoid waxing and waning phases because the Moon doesn't hold the same power at those times.

Step 2

The evenings are usually the best time to create the perfect setting, so around 9 p.m. is a good time.

Step 3

Take care to create the right ambience and mood. Peace and quiet throughout the house is essential.

Step 4

Take five tall white tapered candles into your bathroom and prepare your altar and pentagram. If you have a permanent altar, make it portable for that night, so that you can take it into the bathroom with you. (You will see why in a moment.)

Step 5

Items that should be present on your altar:

- Altar cloth (optional) and pentagram in the center, with the single point facing away from you.
- Five tall white candles, one placed at each point of the pentagram
- One bowl of salt (to the left of the pentagram)
- One bowl of water (to the right of the pentagram)
- A small bowl of earth (at the base of the pentagram)

Place the following around the altar to suit your preference:

- Incense
- A photograph of yourself
- A snippet of your hair
- A handful of flower petals (this is a representation of the earth, so you can use any petals that take your fancy)
- A piece of rose quartz crystal placed on top of your photograph

Step 6

Fill up your bathtub with warm water, add a few drops of rosemary oil and two teaspoons of sea salt, and mix well.

Step 7

Lock the door, light the candles and incense, and turn off the main light.

Step 8

Lie in the bath and inhale the aroma of the oil and incense. Clear your mind and meditate on the fragrance. The following invocation must be memorized (not read) and recited seven times. Look into the burning flames while saying the initiation invocation:

Lead my spirit, oh Angels pure,
Channel my pathway and cleanse my soul.
Angelic light shine down from thee.
With sparkling grace, initiate me.

When you have recited the spell seven times, finish with the words:

So mote it be.

Finally . . . be sure to stay in the bath for about thirty minutes or until you are no longer comfortable. After stepping out of the bathtub and drying yourself, leave the candles to burn for another hour before blowing them out.

Many people experience an uplifting feeling after self-initiation, and many have reported sensing a wonderful spiritual presence for some time afterward.

CHAPTER SIX

A Wiccan Garden

For me, the most wonderful places on Earth are my greenhouse and garden. These are my sanctuary and haven—places where I can truly relax and be at one with nature. I realize that it isn't everyone's idea of heaven, but many witches have an affinity with the garden and with trees and plants in general, so they enjoy an escape to their little plots.

Why Grow Your Own?

Over the years, I have extended my gardening knowledge and gone on to grow all of my own produce from organic seed. For those of you that have never tried this, I wholeheartedly recommend it. When you see the end result, not only do you get an overwhelming sense of fulfillment, but you also get to eat your own produce the very same day that it is plucked from the ground. The taste is so *very* different, the flavors much sharper and intense, and with each mouthful you can be totally assured that no chemicals or unwanted substances have contaminated your food.

From a witchy point of view, there is another crucial reason that I grow all my own produce. Fast food and other pre-packaged meals are created and prepared by strangers. You have no way of knowing what environment your food has been prepared in, nor do you know where the ingredients have come from. I am a firm believer that each and every one of us projects an energy from within, and just as it is so important to be in the right frame of mind when we perform spells and rituals, so is it also vital that we prepare our food when our mood is calm and tranquil. If the guy at the fast-food restaurant has had a fight with his girlfriend, he is guiding his negative energy directly to the food you are about to consume. You may think that this sounds a little far-fetched, but let's face it: moods are renowned for being contagious. If you walk into a room and everyone is laughing, you will automatically start to giggle, even if you missed the joke. The same has to be said if someone is terribly unhappy and is crying. You will inevitably feel sad and may even shed a tear yourself. Goodness knows what may happen to our well-being if we eat food prepared by someone on a lower vibration!

Not only does good, wholesome food give us the right amount of vitamins and nutrients for health, but many ingredients can also work in medicinal and magical ways. With the knowledge that we have inherited from our predecessors, we can use plants and vegetables to our advantage to ward off minor ailments, and we can also use the produce to enhance the spells we cast. Growing herbs is a great way to get started, as these can be germinated on a windowsill in very little time. When they have reached maturity, they can be planted out in the garden, and many will thrive year after year.

Please note that the ancient remedies in this chapter are for information only. I do use some of them myself, but for the purposes of this book, I recommend that you only use these plants on your altar when spell casting, rather than eating them or using them on your skin. Not everyone reacts the same way to different plants, and you certainly don't want an allergic reaction erupting unnecessarily! The same advice applies to any other recipes or applications mentioned in this book—make very sure that they are safe for you to use, and if you are in any doubt, first seek advice from your doctor.

Teas, Tonics, and Superstitions

☛ **Note:** Some plants may be toxic to children and pets. Please check resources to see which ones are and keep such plants out of reach of the ones most vulnerable to their toxic effects.

Aloe Vera

Known for centuries as the "medical plant," aloe vera holds an abundance of healing and nutritional properties, making it famous for curing arthritic swelling, eczema and psoriasis, and for lowering blood sugar in diabetics. This must-have plant is very easy to grow on a windowsill or anywhere light and airy in the home. Just water it once every two weeks and after a while it will produce baby plants, which you can pass on to your family and friends. If you cut the leaf of an aloe vera plant, a jelly-like substance will appear. When rubbed onto the affected area, aloe vera is an effective treatment for burns, scalds, and many other skin conditions. If you don't have the right environment to grow this plant, most popular health food stores and pharmacies sell the gel in tubes, but it is preferable to grow it yourself, for all the reasons that I outlined earlier.

Basil

One of the easiest herbs to grow, basil not only tastes good but has many other uses, both magical and medicinal. Basil is a member of the mint family, and it is famous for its digestive and anti-gas properties. Some herbalists suggest that it is also good for treating stomach cramps, vomiting, constipation, headaches, and anxiety.

The best way to reap the benefits of this herb is to add it to your recipes. You can make an infusion with approximately ten leaves by steeping them in boiling water for five minutes and straining the liquid into a cup. This is a terrific aphrodisiac, so use it if your sex life is flagging or if you want to pep up your partner. Many spells over the years have included basil in fertility rituals. To aid conception, during a full Moon hang a bunch of basil over the bed and make love twice that evening!

Bay Leaves and Berries

Bay leaves and berries fight rheumatism, earaches, and skin rashes. Although we use them widely in our recipes, too many leaves added to an infusion can have the opposite effect and induce vomiting or act as a laxative. This is a commanding herb that is used magically to banish the evil eye and end curses. In Europe, a tied bunch of bay leaves hung above the front door will dispel any unwanted energies. On a more positive note, if the leaves are placed under a pillow, inspiration and prophetic dream sleep will follow.

Catnip

Like basil, catnip is a member of the mint family, and most cats that are fortunate enough to have some growing in their garden worship it. It is quite amusing to watch your cat rolling around in this plant. It obviously provides the cat a "feel-good factor." While I do grow a wealth of this stuff for my furry felines, it has many other uses. A handful of catnip leaves added to the bath is believed to be wonderful for the complexion and also helps to heal skin conditions. Because this herb induces sweating, it is useful for reducing fevers. Tea made with catnip can relieve colds and flu and also helps to put a stop to nausea and diarrhea. To make catnip tea, add two dried teaspoons of the herb to one cup of boiling water and steep for ten minutes. In ancient folklore, catnip was thought to prevent the evil eye, so the tea was given to children with behavioral problems or anxieties.

Chamomile

Chamomile is an annual herb that came from Europe, and it has fantastic healing properties. It is safe for most people to eat the flowers in salads or to infuse them in a warm beverage. The benefits of this herb are many, and it is wonderful for treating stomach ache, hay fever, and insomnia. It is an anti-inflammatory, so use it for arthritis and also for menstrual cramps. Dried chamomile flowers can be made into a potpourri or into herb pillows to help with restful sleep. Scatter the petals around your home, as they will work brilliantly as an insect repellent. This is a great herb to use when casting spells, as it represents calm and peace. For restful sleep, place some chamomile on the altar when you are reciting your invocation, then place it under your pillow at night.

Chives

Chives are rarely mentioned as having any real medicinal properties, but we do know that they are rich in vitamins A and C, which help the blood and circulation. Their magical influences far outweigh their medicinal ones, so chives are used frequently in spells and rituals to chase away evil or negative vibrations. If you feel that someone is sending you ill will or that a bad influence is hanging around your home, hang chives above the front and back doors. They will fend off anyone who has a negative vibration.

Dandelion

Dandelion is reputed to have so many incredible benefits that it is impossible to list them all here, but some of its uses include helping conditions such as constipation, joint pain, and liver dysfunction. In the Middle Ages, people rubbed the plant sap on warts and corns. I tried this on one of my children's warts recently, and I was amazed to find that within a week, the wart had vanished! (Apparently, the inside of a bit of banana skin is also supposed to be a good wart remover.)

Dill

Not only is dill good with fish and salads, but it also works great as a natural remedy for the treatment of hiccups, menstrual cramps, flatulence, and flu. If you have any of these problems, add dill to your daily diet and you will soon start to reap the benefits. The seeds can also work as a diuretic and stimulate the appetite after a bout of illness. Carrying a few sprigs of dill on your person is said to magically bring romance into your life. Nibbling some of the fresh leaves sweetens the breath and sends out a message that you want to be kissed.

Evening Primrose

Evening primrose has a long history as an alternative medicine. This plant can be found all over the world, usually growing along the roadside or in gardens. It is understood to have a positive effect on cholesterol problems and is useful for treating menopausal symptoms, pain, and inflammation. Used externally, it keeps your skin in good condition, and it is also absorbed into the body this way. The leaves can be cooked and eaten as greens and the roots are said to be sweet when boiled. You can also use the seeds to dust the top of your bread by roasting them in the oven for twenty minutes at 350 degrees Fahrenheit. Evening primrose oil is also available from most health food shops.

Feverfew

Grown in the garden, feverfew is a must if you suffer from repeated headaches or migraine. Be warned though: It is best to contain this plant in a pot, as it can spread and grow out of control. You can make feverfew tea by putting one tablespoon of the fresh leaves or one teaspoon of dried leaves in a ceramic cup with boiling water. Infuse the liquid for three minutes and then pour it through a strainer. Because feverfew can be bitter, you might want to add a teaspoon of honey to sweeten the tea. Another good way to prevent headaches from occurring is to eat three of the fresh leaves daily in a sandwich.

Garlic

Garlic is said to be great for warding off vampires, but a more realistic use is to eat some daily to help maintain a healthy body. Try some every day to fend off colds or flu, but if you can't stand the taste, get some "one-a-day" garlic capsules from a drugstore.

Ginseng

Ginseng is said to encourage general well-being, and it can help you to relax when you are feeling tense or agitated. Native Americans recognized this as a highly effective magical plant and used it as a love medicine. To bring home a wayward partner, an individual would rub the plant onto his or her body and clothes. For a general tonic, boil five to eight slices of the ginseng root in a pot for about ten minutes. The longer the ginseng bubbles, the stronger the tea will be, so if you really need to loosen up, boil it for a few extra minutes. Strain the tea into a cup and enjoy.

Heather

It is said that heather is the flower of the fairies and that within its foliage, a secret portal links the fairy world with our own. If this plant is growing in your garden, witches' lore holds that you will be protected from misfortune and will live a long and healthy life. Many witches like to dry heather and hang bunches, tied with pretty ribbons, in their windows for luck.

Ivy

Ivy growing on the outside walls of a house is believed to be a deterrent against misfortune, but if you cut down the plant, its luck will be removed and you will be sure to change address.

Jasmine

Jasmine is used as a remedy for treating dry, irritated, and sensitive skin. The oils can be extracted from the plant to prevent muscle spasms and to relieve sprains. For centuries, the Chinese have infused the dried flowers with cocoa, which is said to create a drink that induces peaceful sleep. Jasmine is also used magically as a seduction herb. To get your partner in the mood, pop a handful of fresh jasmine flowers into your lover's underwear drawer. Light a white candle and say the name of your partner seven times. When the candle has burned down, passion will follow. Be warned though: There is nothing romantic about this spell—just pure, lusty fun!

Lavender

How wonderful it is to see row after row of this wonderful herb extending out before your eyes. Its soft purple haze and pungent fragrance hang in the air, calming and pacifying the senses. For centuries it has been used to cleanse and protect, clearing homes of bad vibrations, and medicinally, to induce sleep. To ease the pain of headaches or migraines naturally, rub a few drops of pure lavender oil into the temples. For insomnia, a few drops sprinkled onto your pillow at night will send you gently into dream sleep. Rubbing it into the wrists of family members will magically soothe any friction between parent and child or between siblings. No home should be without a bottle of this oil, as its properties are so remarkable. For many years, my friend Sasha has infused lavender plants in small bottles of oil. She rubs the lavender oil on her hands and her daughter's hands to relieve rheumatoid arthritis.

Lovage Root

Lovage root tea lessens bloating and flatulence, and combined with other herbs, such as mint and chamomile, it can counteract cold and flu symptoms. A few of the leaves infused in boiling water and then drained will also work as an excellent diuretic. An old remedy to alleviate blotches or boils is to bruise lovage leaves and fry them in a little lard. While the leaves are still hot (but not hot enough to burn the skin), lay them over the spot or boil, and the compress will quickly dispel infection. In rituals, lovage lives up to its name, as it is outstanding for attracting lovers or romance. On a full Moon, burn the dried leaves in a flameproof dish in the garden while chanting any love spell.

☛ **Note:** Lovage should *not* be consumed during pregnancy or if you have kidney disease. Always check with your doctor before taking lovage.

Marjoram

Marjoram is a sweetly scented herb that is said to relieve toothache. Years ago, it was thought that if you chewed the leaves, the toothache pain would ease, although having good strong teeth, I have never tried this method of pain relief. Make a lucky talisman or charm from the leaves and root of marjoram to enhance peace within friendships and to protect marriages from infidelity.

Mint

Mint has many different varieties, but peppermint is the most efficient to use for medicinal purposes. A hot cup of peppermint tea is a fantastic way to settle the stomach after a big meal, and it can relieve painful trapped wind after surgery. Its vapors are reputed to relieve sinus and nasal problems. The spirits are said to love the scent of mint, so I always have a little pot of fresh leaves on my altar whenever I cast a spell for money, study, or psychic vision.

Oregano

Oregano was traditionally famous in Greece for treating aching muscles, whereas in China it was used as a cure for fever. The oil found in its leaves works largely as an analgesic for tender teeth or gums, but it has many other medicinal uses. Infusions of the herb calm menstrual pain, nervousness, headaches, and bronchitis. Superstition has it that drinking three cups or more of oregano tea a day helps to heal a broken heart. To make oregano tea, pour a cup of boiling water over one full teaspoon of the dried herb or five fresh leaves. Let it brew for ten minutes, then filter the infusion.

Parsley

Parsley leaves are said to work naturally as a diuretic and to help cleanse and relieve the liver and kidneys. Parsley is also understood to be the only plant that, if chewed, will take the smell of garlic from your breath. If you are madly in love, don't cut parsley with a knife, as you will cut your love as well. Rip the parsley into small pieces—it is much safer!

Rosemary

Rosemary is one of my favorite herbs, not just because it tastes great with lamb, but because of its many health benefits. One of its appealing factors is that it is said to possess antioxidant properties, which help to prevent cancer. Ancient myth also states that rubbing the essential oil into the scalp will cure alopecia, but I don't know how true this is. From a magical point of view, rosemary is a binding herb. If you weave three long sprigs of the herb together and chant your lover's name over and over, you and your lover will remain together in this life and the next. Burning dried rosemary will enhance mental alertness and give you a better memory, so it is wonderful for performing spells to help you to pass exams and driving tests.

☛ **Note:** Don't take rosemary as a medicinal remedy if you are epileptic.

Sage

Sage has superb antiseptic properties, and sage tea is often used as a gargle to treat sore throat. New research also shows that sage tea could be beneficial to people with diabetes if taken in conjunction with their insulin. (Check with your doctor first.) To make the tea, steep one teaspoon of dried sage or six fresh sage leaves in boiling water for ten minutes. Strain and drink the infusion. Compressed dried sage leaves are often called smudging sticks. Native Americans burn the sweet-smelling sage to ward off evil. I use sage this way once a month to clear any negative vibes I may have in my home, or to cleanse my home if anyone has been ill.

Saint John's Wort (Hypericum)

Saint John's Wort was once thought to rid the body of evil spirits, so it is no surprise that this herb is used today to treat mild depression. It is one of the most commonly purchased herbal products in the United States, but it should be taken only with the guidance of a doctor or someone who is really knowledgeable about herbal products. Magically, it is also used to reverse negative energies and to quiet down fractious situations. If you have families at war, bury twelve leaves in a pot of soil and place it outside the front door.

Sorrel

Sorrel has a bitter taste, so if it is being used for culinary purposes, you may want to mask the flavor by combining it with sweeter ingredients. A potion of chopped sorrel leaves and vinegar is used medicinally to rub onto the skin as a cure for ringworm. Wine made from the flowers may ease ulcerated bowels and help to cure kidney stones. In spell making, sorrel is used as a main representative for any health rituals. Scatter the leaves and flowers on the altar when your spell is underway.

Thyme

Thyme can work well as an antifungal agent. Cover two ounces of the fresh leaves with alcohol. Place the infusion in a glass jar and tighten the lid well. Leave for twenty-four hours, and then dab the liquid sparingly on the affected area. Thyme can cause adverse reactions, so be sure to use only a little. Thyme and time do go hand in hand, so if you need a spell to give you more time to complete tasks, run a bath, holding thyme leaves under the running water, and have a soak.

☛ **Note:** Although thyme is generally considered safe to eat, strong medicinal uses of this herb should be avoided if you are pregnant. As usual, always first check with your doctor or a qualified herbal practitioner if there is any doubt whatsoever.

Valerian

Valerian has calming effects, and its mild sedative quality can promote sleep. It also helps to prevent anxiety. I use this herb more for magical purposes to calm down aggressive situations. When the plant is in flower, boil a handful of its petals in a pan with three cups of water. When the potion has cooled, remove the petals and pour the liquid onto your front doorstep or on the ground directly in front of the entryway to your home. Everyone who enters your home will be sweetness personified!

Ground valerian root makes a wonderful nerve treatment and also a sedative, but it is dangerous to drink too much of it. Valerian is known to be an herb of the planet Mercury, and any astrologer can tell you that Mercury rules the nervous system.

☛ **Note:** Do not bathe in this herb's oils if you have any skin disorders. Valerian must be kept away from children and pets.

CHAPTER SEVEN

Animal Magic

For many of us, animals play an important role in our day-to-day lives. Pets are a part of the family. We name them, love them, and nurture them. Because most White Witches have a passionate love of nature and all things living, we believe that there is equality between animals and us, making them just as important as our fellow humans. Our pets are the spokespeople for the animal kingdom, and they are given to us so that we may understand their vibration. Humans on a spiritual pathway now have a better understanding of pet care, which has enabled them to empathize with all creatures. An important thing to remember is that animals have no karma. Unlike us, they don't need to keep reincarnating to improve their vibration. It is imperative that we cause no suffering to them, and if we cannot help to improve their conditions in a practical manner, then we must ask the angels to intercede and go to their aid.

Living so far out in the country and away from the hustle and bustle of the town, I have been able to study the wildlife and farm animals in my area. It is quite amazing how all the different species interact and communicate, not just with one another, but with people as well. I have a lake on my land that each year gets overgrown with large sprawling reeds. One summer, I took out my little rowboat to try and thin out the foliage. I was chopping away when out of nowhere a fine looking lady dragonfly flew in front of my face. She was making such a fuss and commotion that if she had been human, she would have been shouting at full volume. The impression I got was that she was pleading with me to be careful. For the next ten minutes, she would fly away for a few seconds and then return, flitting backward and forward as if asking me to follow her. I stopped what I was doing and decided to investigate what she was so anxious about. Glancing up, I saw high on one of the reeds a little bundle of her eggs. She fluttered onto the reed and continued to buzz at me. Telepathically, I told her not to worry and I left the lake.

We don't give our planetary creatures the credit they deserve. Their intelligence is second to none. They are obviously not able to speak our language, but they do communicate with us in the best way they know how.

I have a special connection with birds. Our feathered friends are messengers, so they always make a dramatic entrance when something important is about to happen. I am quite superstitious about birds flying into the house, because each time this has happened to me, news of a death has soon followed. The situation isn't the same for everyone, but it is usually the case that when you encounter a wild bird in unusual circumstances, some news will reach you in a matter of days. Birds also know who is sensitive to them and who is not. As a young girl, I lived in the middle of a busy city in the industrial north of England. One morning I was chatting to our neighbor in the front garden when a parakeet flew over and landed on my head. Needless to say, the budgie knew that I would go out and purchase a cage, fill it with food, toys, and bells, and make it my absolute mission to provide him a good home! After all, he could have landed on anyone's head in the street, but he chose to land on mine. Shortly afterward, we discovered that an aviary had blown down in the wind a few miles away, so we were able to reunite Bobbie the budgie with his owner.

Most White Witches have an affinity with creatures. Cats occupy a special place in our hearts and have been known throughout time as the witch's familiar. Felines know when they are in the presence of a White Witch, and they will follow on the heels of someone who they feel is on a spiritual pathway. Some people find cats hard to love, perhaps because they kill birds. This can be difficult for some people to understand, especially when the "killer cat" has only recently been fed a large helping of designer cat food. We must understand the instincts of cats and the fact that, even though we call them our pets, they are in fact wild animals that choose to be with us. They are free to leave whenever they want, and while most of them know which side their bread is buttered on, they can sometimes get lost or trapped and then need to survive on birds, rats, and small creatures for a while.

All animals, from insects to giant bears, are recognized within the White Witch family. If you have a special relationship with a certain type of animal, this is called your "power animal" and will be a wonderful representative to focus on when spell casting. If you are on a higher level of spirituality, you will naturally understand and love the animal vibration, especially cats!

A Magical Moment of Joy

I have often believed in the philosophy of "moments of joy," and I would like to share this particular one with you:

I had agreed to house-sit for Mamma while she was away on holiday. One mild evening, I decided to sit on her garden bench while enjoying a chicken sandwich. From the side of her garden, a beautiful vixen peeped out of the bushes, then sped away. I was completely taken aback! She appeared nervous, but she approached again, probably spurred on by the smell of the chicken sandwich. She brazenly walked up to me and sat down in front of me, like a begging dog. Tentatively I held out a piece of my sandwich, which she immediately took, along with an accidental nip of my index finger, before she ran off again.

Some weeks later, Mamma and my stepfather had returned home after a day out at a wildlife sanctuary. Relaxing in the lounge later that evening, they were chatting about the day while enjoying a glass of wine. The back door was open because they were waiting for the cats to come in from the garden. After a short while the cats strolled in, jumped into their bed, and cuddled down to sleep.

What happened next was so amazing that I still can hardly believe it. In the open doorway of the sitting room appeared the beautiful vixen, calmly surveying the room and its occupants. Mamma whispered to my stepfather to get the camera, and soon he was rapidly taking photographs. Mamma lifted the phone, pressed the button for my number, and spoke softly into the receiver: "Leanna, you'll never believe this, but a wild fox is in the family room!"

Nearby she had some potato chips in a bowl, and the fox came closer as she offered one of them to her. In the next second, the vixen had stretched up onto Mamma's knee and snatched the chip from her fingers. We knew she could nip, so Mamma prayed the vixen wouldn't bite her. She gazed into the fox's golden eyes and the vixen looked back at her with total trust, her muzzle less than five inches from Mamma's face, asking for more chips.

Mamma offered the vixen another and told the vixen to take it gently. After three of four times, the fox got the hang of taking the chip without biting any fingers. When she had her fill, she decided to explore the lounge, jumping onto the armchair and looking underneath a lamp. Electricity was obviously new and fascinating territory for her. Next she spotted the television and watched, enraptured, as the newscaster reported on the events of the day. Then, as all wild animals do, she decided that she must return to her home and the fields at the bottom of the garden.

For the next three months, the vixen came every evening at the same time and happily ate a bowl of dog food. Once, she encountered the cats and brought her bushy tail around her in a threatening stance, chattering in a strange way. She was told in no uncertain terms to "Stop it!" This she did quite sheepishly, and she ignored the cats from that day on. My stepfather taught her to play with a Ping-Pong ball on a string. Often she would come in if we had company and allow other people to feed her. The most bizarre experience occurred when two good friends were over for supper. The vixen strolled into the dining room and sat very quietly next to a chair, begging for a titbit, which, of course, she got! It felt as if we had a little family dog in the place; however, she was neither a dog nor a cat, but a mixture of the two—very intelligent, very mischievous, and very special.

Mamma framed a picture of the vixen and put it on the wall unit in the lounge for all to see. One morning, she came into the room and saw the picture face down on the floor. Our hearts sank; we knew it was a bad omen, and a terrible sadness washed over us.

Mamma says, "Each second she was with us was a magical moment, never to be taken for granted." We didn't see her after that, but we have the memories and, of course, the photographs. We feel so blessed to have been given the privilege of this encounter with nature.

CHAPTER EIGHT

Tarot Magic

The subject of tarot is extensive and can be complex, but I will keep this chapter as simple as possible. Countless people who are keen to learn about the esoteric become interested in exploring the ancient art of tarot, and it is quite likely that you already have some knowledge of the cards. Tarot cards can be used to give a spell more potency. You should be aware that each of the seventy-eight cards in a tarot deck has a specific meaning. Some hold more significance than others, and some are more dominant than others. When we look into the subject of tarot magic, it is always best to use these governing cards. Some cards are not suitable to use with tarot magic; for that reason I have listed only the ones that you will need (in the table on the facing page).

There are thousands of different tarot packs in circulation today and it really doesn't matter which deck you decide to use; all tarot cards hold a magic of their own, and they can all help to bring about a positive result to your spells. Choose a deck that visually "speaks" to you, one to which you are attracted.

First, you need to arrange your altar, placing all your chosen items on its surface. Using one to three tarot cards per spell is usually best, and these cards can be placed anywhere on the table where there is room. Four or more cards could confuse the ritual, so less is best. For example, if you wanted to attract romance into your life, you would set out all the necessary items and add the Lovers card to the collection. For spells for those who wish to conceive a child, the Empress would be appropriate, as this is the card of pregnancy and motherhood. For those who know absolutely nothing about the tarot, I have noted the relevant cards to use with certain spells.

Tarot Card	Key Meaning
The Magician	Developing psychic abilities
The High Priestess	Spiritual protection; communicating with a female on the other side
The Empress	Fertility and motherhood
The Emperor	Legal or business dealings
The Lovers	Affairs of the heart and love affairs
The Chariot	Travel, movement, and changes
Strength	Health and strength in all areas of life; kindness to animals
The Hermit	Spiritual protection or communicating with a spirit guide
Justice	Legal situations
Temperance	Regain patience and angelic help
The Star	Communicate with your angels
The Moon	Deception; discover if someone is lying to you
The Sun	Bring about a joyous situation
The World	Travel abroad
Ace of Cups	Bring about happy outcome; births and babies
Two of Cups	Engagements and marriages; soul mates and love
Three of Cups	Happy celebrations; family get-togethers
Five of Cups	Connect with someone in your past
Six of Cups	Reconciliations
Seven of Cups	Making the right choices/decisions; information during sleep
Eight of Cups	Strength to move away from negative situations
Nine of Cups	Wishes and dreams to be fulfilled
Ace of Wands	New jobs; fertility; travel
Three of Wands	Improvements in careers
Six of Wands	Awaiting news; victory in projects
Eight of Wands	Journey by plane and new irons in the fire
Six of Swords	Moving house and travel
Ace of Pentacles	Money luck and putting an end to financial problems
Eight of Pentacles	Successfully completing courses or passing exams; new jobs
Nine of Pentacles	Bringing about a better financial situation; long journeys
Ten of Pentacles	Happy marriages and inheritances
Ace of Swords	Taking control; preventing a situation from getting out of control
Four of Swords	Recovery from illness

If you want to perform a spell for someone you know, it is a good idea to have a representation of that person on your altar. You may not be able to obtain a photograph of the individual, but you could use any of the court cards from a tarot deck to represent the person. The court cards are the kings, queens, knights, and pages, and each has its own hair and eye coloring, so do your best to match the card with the person.

AGE RANGES

Kings	Men of age 29 and over
Queens	Women and mature teenage girls
Knights	Young men between the ages of 17 and 29
Pages	Male or female children from birth to 15 years of age

COLORS AND SIGNIFICATOR CARDS

You can use coloring and significator cards to represent a person by his or her birth sign if you know it, or you can use the old gypsy method, which means that you select a card that matches the inquirer's coloring.

Cups	Water signs: Cancer, Scorpio, Pisces; blue to hazel eyes, light to brown hair
Wands	Fire signs: Aries, Leo, Sagittarius; blue or green eyes, fair skin, fair to red hair
Swords	Air signs: Gemini, Libra, Aquarius; hazel or dark eyes, dark hair, olive or black skin
Pentacles	Earth signs: Taurus, Virgo, Capricorn; any color eyes, brown or black hair

We can see that if you wanted to cast a spell for your daughter who was born under the sign of Virgo, the Queen or Page of Pentacles would be an appropriate card to represent her on your altar. If your inquirer was a Leo male, you would use the King of Wands to represent him.

Spells for all Seasons

You can mix and match cards as required. Here are just a few examples:

Spells to Increase Psychic Vision

The Magician
The High Priestess
The High Priest or Hierophant

Spells for Pregnancy and Motherhood

The Empress
The Two of Cups
The Ace of Cups
The Sun
Any of the Pages

Spells to Sell or Move House

The Hierophant
The Eight of Rods
The Six of Swords

Spells for Romance and Love

The Two of Cups
The Lovers
The Ace of Cups

Spells for Work and Business

The Ace of Wands
Strength
The Ace of Pentacles

Spells for Legal Problems

Justice
The Emperor
The Ace of Cups
The Ace of Pentacles

Spells for Money

The Ace of Pentacles
The Ace of Cups
The Sun
The Wheel of Fortune

Examples of Tarot Spells

Here are two sample spells to show you how tarot cards can be used in magic.

Communicate with Your Angel

If life is getting you down and you want to contact your angel for help, this simple candle spell can open the lines of communication. You can cast this spell on any day of the week.

Set up a small altar and place the High Priestess and the Magician cards on the surface. Next inscribe your name with a sharp knife onto a purple candle, and add the words "To contact my angel." Sit quietly for a few minutes and light the candle next to your cards. Try to visualize yourself in a beautiful, tranquil place. Imagine that your guardian angel is with you, subconsciously ask for his or her protection, and then say this incantation:

I summon my Angel guide
To bless me with your love.
Let my mind be open to your message.

Then chant the following three times:

Visit me in dreams so deep
So you may speak while I'm asleep.

Let the candle burn for an hour before blowing it out. You can repeat this spell, using the same candle, as often as you like. Many people experience a different frame of mind after a night's sleep.

A Spell for Good Health

We all fall ill from time to time, and, although magic rarely cures an illness, it can help to alleviate the symptoms.

YOU WILL NEED

A bowl of salt
A piece of citrine crystal
Two white candles
From a tarot deck, the Sun and the Ace of Cups cards

Sprinkle a large handful of the salt in a large circle on the floor. Light the candles anywhere nearby and sit crossed-legged inside the circle. Place the Ace of Cups and the Sun directly in front of you. Holding the citrine to your forehead, say these words three times:

Light my soul with radiant grace.
The rays of the Sun, upon my face
All the illness will dispel.
I shall now be fit and well.

Stay in the circle for about ten minutes and imagine yourself getting better. When you want to leave the circle, thank your angels and be sure to keep the citrine in your pocket for the rest of the day.

CHAPTER NINE

Magnetic Magic

It is a fact that Earth is surrounded by magnetic fields, and although we are all aware of the power that a magnet possesses, we also need to understand the amazing impact it can have on our lives where magic is concerned. Magical magnets have been used for thousands of years in Africa, Greece, India, Egypt, and China. Many cultures throughout time have sought out the power of the magnet and used it alongside rituals to heal the sick. Even Cleopatra is said to have worn a lodestone (magnetic iron ore) on her forehead to prevent aging.

Unlike some prescription drugs, magnets will not harm you. Today, many alternative therapists swear by magneto-therapy. It is supposed that when we use magnets to help to cure health issues, our blood circulation improves. This in turn encourages a healthier metabolism and leads to a better overall physical condition. However, as wonderful as a magnet may be, it cannot heal all health problems. Below are some conditions that may show improvement with a magnet, plus a few tips on using magnets magically.

> **Warning:** DO NOT place magnets on your body or use these spells if you wear a heart pacemaker, have metallic mesh coronary stents, or have any other metallic devices anywhere in your body without first consulting your doctor.

Chronic Fatigue

Fatigue affects all of us at some time in our lives, whether it is from overwork or simply from periodic bouts of insomnia, which affect many of us at some time in our lives. Place a large magnet under your mattress for three nights, and notice how much better you sleep. You can also purchase magnetic toppers for your mattress, which are renowned for preventing stiffness of the joints.

Arthritis and Joint Pain

The power of two small round magnets affixed to the affected area with surgical tape will lessen joint pain. This technique really works if you have a knee problem. For best results, attach the magnets before bedtime for a couple of weeks, and the swelling will go down. This method can be used in the same way for back conditions.

Eczema, Toothache, Headache/Migraine, and Earache

Health problems associated with the area from the neck upward particularly benefit from magnetic jewelry. A necklace or earrings made from magnets can really make a difference. You can find these items easily in online stores and some esoteric supply shops.

Here is a story about toothache and magnets. One day, my friend Eva's husband, Robert, came down with toothache, and as is always the case with toothache, this happened at an inconvenient time. It was a long holiday weekend, and Eva and Robert were away at a psychic fair. Robert knew he could consult his dentist during the following week, but in the meantime, he had to work and be pleasant to people despite his pain. A man who was treating people with acupuncture at the event offered to place a magnet on each of Robert's ears as a temporary solution. Robert was happy for the man to try this, and soon he sported two tiny magnets—not much larger than pinheads—fixed to parts of his ears with tiny circles of Scotch tape. To Robert's amazement and relief, the pain disappeared and didn't return at all!

Feet

For those who suffer with foot problems such as gout and plantar warts, try wearing magnetic insoles in your shoes, as this practice has proved successful in reducing these conditions.

Spells and Magnets

We know that magnets possess powerful properties, and when they are used without any additional treatments, they can work successfully. However, when the magnet is used in harmony with a spell or ritual, the potency almost triples.

Tummy Trouble

Thousands of women all over the world are cursed with menstrual problems, stomach cramps, and PMS. This spell operates by twinning angelic intervention with the Earth's power. Many women who have performed this spell have reported feeling much better in no time at all. You can also use this spell if you have any abdominal condition such as prostate trouble, stomach ulcers, or irritable bowel syndrome.

YOU WILL NEED

- Three small magnets of any shape
- Three white candles

- A small piece of clean amethyst crystal
- A small glass of pure bottled water
- Lavender oil

Set out an altar in your bedroom and place all of the above items on the surface. Drop the piece of amethyst into the glass of water, then go take a long leisurely bath. When you are totally relaxed, get out of the bath, light the three candles, and lie on your bed. Massage a few drops of the lavender oil into the pelvic or stomach area before placing the three magnets on your tummy. If a particular spot within your abdomen is especially painful, be sure to rest the magnet directly on it.

Close your eyes and concentrate on your abdomen for about fifteen minutes.

Now invoke your angel to heal you with the magnets. Say three times:

Angel Goddess, beauteous light,
Magnetic power comes into sight.
Draw upon the Moon for me
To banish pain, so mote it be.

Lie quietly for a few more minutes and then remove the amethyst from the glass. Wash your face with the magical water in the morning to complete your spell.

Health-related issues are not the only things that can be improved with magnetic magic; magnets, if prepared properly, can make great amulets and talismans, inviting all sorts of positive luck to come your way.

Note: Remember that there is no substitute for professional guidance. If you have pain or any other symptoms that are cause for concern, you must visit your doctor and follow his or her advice. If you choose to take any additional steps, such as methods outlined in this book, ensure that you discuss them with your doctor first. Even if these recipes and other forms of alternative support aren't harmful in themselves, they could interfere with your doctor's formal treatment, and your doctor is the only person who can judge whether or not this is the case.

Money Tips

To enhance your money energy, fold in half a dollar bill, a five-pound note, or a note in whatever currency you use. Sandwich the money between two magnets about one inch in diameter each. Keep this money sandwich in your bag or pocket at all times. Within a short space of time, you will find bits of money coming in from all directions. Also, if you run a business and want to improve your earnings, place a magnet of any size near or beside your cash register to attract cash.

WARNINGS

- Never leave a magnet in your wallet, as it is known to wipe all information from your credit cards. Don't place a magnet on top of your television. It will affect the picture quality.
- Never place a magnet near video recorders or audiocassettes or anywhere near your computer. Important information is likely to be erased.

Does He Like Me?

If you need to know how someone feels about you but are afraid to ask, or if you have romantic feelings for someone but need to know whether he or she feels the same, try this: Light a red candle while holding a large magnet, and say:

Goddess of the Moon and skies,
Engulf this magic before my eyes.
Romantic times, come hither, come near.
With this magnet make it clear.

The next part of the spell is tricky, but because it works, it is worth a try.

While the candle is burning, cover the magnet with a dish towel. Hit it with a hammer so it splits in two. Alternatively, you can cut the magnet in half using a tile cutter. Keep one half for yourself and give the other half to the person you like. Tell the object of your affection to keep it on his or her person at all times.

Make no contact with the individual for one week. (He or she can contact you, but you must not initiate the contact.) On the day you see each other again, fish out your magnet and ask to see your potential lover's. If he or she produces it, put the two halves together again and give the magnet to the individual for luck. Within one month, one of you will find the courage to ask the other out on a date. If the other person fails to produce his or her half of the magnet, it is doubtful that a relationship will develop.

Magnetic Sand

Magnetic sand is supposed to be extremely lucky if carried in a red bag. It also works brilliantly for practicing witches who like to cast a circle before performing spells. Sprinkle a handful of the magnetic sand on the ground in the shape of a circle, then step into the circle to carry out the ritual. If you have trouble sourcing the sand, file about six thin magnets down to make your own.

Stress Buster

A magnet is a great stress buster, and it helps to overcome panic attacks and depression. When we are constantly worrying, we can become so absorbed in our own anxiety that it affects our way of thinking and causes our chakras to become out of balance. By using the following type of magic, our seven internal chakras can be once again realigned, and our general mental well-being restored.

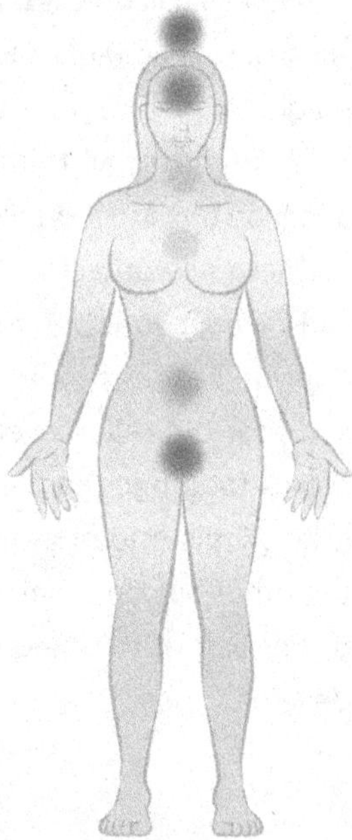

- Cleanse seven small magnets by leaving them in a bowl of salt overnight. Lie flat on your bed and, starting from the top of your head, place the magnets on the points indicated in the diagram.
- Lie on the bed with the magnets on your chakras for thirty minutes each day. Within a week, you will start to feel your troubles and hassles fading.

Magnificent Tips for the Home and Garden

Magnets can be used around the home and garden to reduce your energy bills. Lime scale is a huge problem in some areas; it reduces the efficiency of heating elements and clogs pipes and shower heads. Attaching a magnet to your water pipe may substantially decrease the build-up of lime scale.

- If your houseplants are wilting, bury a small magnet of any shape in the soil, and within a few weeks the foliage on your plant will be lush and lavish.
- A couple of magnets attached to your garden hose will produce more radiant growth in your flowers.
- A large horseshoe magnet buried in your garden makes the soil more fertile for growing vegetables.

Animal Magnetism

At least one company specializes in manufacturing magnetic products specifically designed for use with animals. It produces collars for cats and dogs and leg supports for horses. The magnets have an effect on illnesses such as arthritis, and many animal owners have been astounded at the collar's effects. If this technique interests you, search the Internet for a source of these items in your area. Magnetic collars also work brilliantly for nervous or temperamental pets. They calm the pets' anxieties and are thought to make them more sociable.

Cast a Spell Using your Appliances

Many White Witches notice that their spells have an enhanced performance when they are conducted near appliances such as microwaves and washing machines. This is because these appliances

have electromagnetic fields. When the microwave or washing machine is working and a spell is being performed nearby, the power from the appliance combined with the force of the ritual make the end result quite dynamic.

A Quick Electro-Magnetic Spell to Protect Your Home

Mix a teaspoon of earth from your garden into a large cup of tap water. Add one teaspoon of salt to the cup, then place the cup inside your microwave. Light a white tea-light candle and place it on top of the microwave. Set the microwave on high for one minute (keep an eye on it in case the water boils) and say the following seven times:

Earth and salt, water pure,
Keep all evil from my door.

Next, dig a small hole in the garden and pour the heated contents of the cup into the ground. If you don't have a garden, you can place the finished spell in a flowerpot outside your front door. For an extra blessing, let the candle burn down and go out. This spell will dispel any negativity that others may have sent you.

CHAPTER TEN

The Power of the Pendulum

The pendulum is often used by dowsers or water diviners, and it provides an acceptable alternative to divining rods. A pendulum has various other uses, such as discovering the sex of an unborn baby, finding lost objects, and diagnosing illness. With practice, it can go one step further and provide a psychic channel, making it possible to communicate directly with your guide or angel.

You don't need to buy an expensive pendulum. You can make one quite simply by tying a ring or any other small object to a length of string. Indeed, a friend of mine uses an acorn! There are no rules governing the length of the string, but somewhere between twelve and twenty inches will work best. For centuries, poorer witches have used wooden pendulums, or buttons or a needle threaded onto a piece of cotton. Modern witches prefer to work with pendulums made from crystals, which come in many variations, such as rose quartz, citrine, and amethyst, and which are often attached to a long silver chain. I find cyrstals helpful for pinpointing problem areas on the body, and when exercised accurately, crystals can align the chakras and heal the mental state, as well as physical ailments.

Once you have your pendulum, it is a good idea to charge it. To do this, leave the object outside overnight to soak up the Moon's rays. For crystal pendulums, you can perform a cleansing and blessing procedure by leaving the crystal in a bowl of salt water for a few hours. This will remove any negativity left in the crystal by those who might have handled it before you.

When using the pendulum, hold the end of the string or chain lightly between your thumb and forefinger, supporting your elbow on a hard surface to limit your arm's movement. To begin, you should "test" the pendulum by asking a question to which you know the answer is "yes." The pendulum will start to rotate, either in a clockwise or counterclockwise direction, or it might make a back and forth or right to left movement. Whichever it is, the motion will be your sign for "yes." Once you have established this, ask for the "no" signal in the same way.

When I use the pendulum, my signal for "yes" is clockwise movement; "no" is signified by counterclockwise movement. When the pendulum doesn't know the answer, it either stays very still or it swings randomly. Each person is individual and each pendulum is unique, so you will have to interpret the signs for yourself. This will be the first initiation into getting to know your pendulum.

Be sure to ask the pendulum specific questions that require yes or no answers. When you have finished, it is good to give this magical tool its own resting place, such as a nice velvet-lined box or wrapped in a colorful piece of silk. I have a wooden birdcage hanging from the ceiling in my sun room, and I loop the pendulum onto the cage to catch the sun's rays.

Dictionary Divination

Dictionary divination is one of my favorite forms of divination, and I use it on a regular basis when I need to know the outcome of a situation. All you need is a large dictionary and a little patience. The dictionary works as a tool for contact and communication with higher level guides, and it is a bit like a portal between this world and the next. The messages can be specific, and they usually are accurate. This is so much the case that after twenty years of working this way, I have found that it has rarely failed me. It can give names and times and an insight into the future.

Before you begin to experiment with it, you need to sit quietly and ask for spiritual protection. As in any form of spirit communication, it is easy to accidentally tap into the lower vibrations, so you need to be sure that you are conversing with a positive spirit rather than a negative one. Just ask your angel to encircle you in light and to focus on all things good. Ask for protection and true divination and always thank your angel afterward. It can take a few minutes for the link to be made, so please be patient. If you get muddled messages that make no sense, this means that the spirit world doesn't want to talk to you at that time. It's best to respect this and try again a few days later.

To begin, flick the pages of the dictionary with your thumb while asking your question out loud, without looking at the pages. Then, still not looking down, point your finger randomly at an open page. Read the word that appears under your finger; if it doesn't make sense as an answer to your question, try looking a few lines above or below. It might take ten minutes or so for you to establish communication with your guide, so be persistent and don't give up. You will know if you have encountered a negative spirit, because everything you read will be doom and gloom or just crude. If this happens, tell it quite clearly to go away and then go through the protection scenario again. To be honest, this negative interference doesn't happen often.

A Personal Story

A few years ago, I lost my house keys. I didn't panic at first, but after three days of turning the house upside down and not being able to go out, I began to worry. I decided to try to communicate with the spirit world through the dictionary, to see whether I could get an idea where the keys might be. I flicked the pages, asking out loud, "Please tell me where my keys are." After a few attempts, my finger rested on the word "wardrobe." I quickly dashed up the stairs and ransacked the closet. Finding nothing, I asked again. This time my finger pointed to the word "denim." The first thing that sprang to mind was that the keys might be in my jeans pocket, but I hit a dead end again, as the jeans were in the laundry basket! By now I was getting fed up. I asked once more, and the spirit world responded with the word "back." So I ventured up the stairs again and started to go through every item of clothing that I possessed. Tucked underneath a coat was an old denim jacket that I had worn a few days earlier, and there, inside the pocket, were my elusive keys!

On another occasion, I mislaid my datebook. I am lost without it, because I have most of my life planned at least six months ahead. I asked the dictionary to tell me in which room my datebook was. It said, "sitting room." I asked, "Where in the sitting room?" It replied, "Unit." I scanned the wall unit thoroughly, but there was still no sign of the missing book. I returned to the dictionary again and my finger came up with "behind."

Sure enough, the diary had fallen behind the wall unit and was resting on the baseboard. As you can imagine, my relief was immense, and I gave a hearty thank you to my spiritual helpers.

CHAPTER ELEVEN

Love Spells

Let's face it: Ideally, each and every one of us would like to be in a wonderful, caring relationship. Some people spend their entire lives searching for that elusive individual, entering and leaving many love affairs and marriages before finding the right one! Some meet their perfect partner straightaway and remain in a relationship 'til death them do part, but others are not so fortunate. A very small minority of people will go one step further and dust off their pentagram to cast a spell for a beloved.

Although I am certainly not against this practice, there are rules to follow when dealing with matters of the heart. Love spells must be approached with great caution, or the long-term consequences can be devastating. One of the main laws within the White Witch community is that we must not under any circumstances set out to influence the heart or mind of another person. Meddling with the way others think and feel will indirectly put them in a vulnerable position and interfere with their karma. Whether for a few short months or a lifetime commitment, each relationship that we find ourselves in is part of our destiny, and each is spiritually planned. Romantic encounters teach us much about our inner selves, and if at some stage we decide that a union has run its course, we have the choice and free will to move away from it. This can be a real problem when people cast spells to win back lovers.

Let us now look at an example of karmic intervention.

A woman leaves her marriage because she is terribly unhappy. She has realized after ten years that she doesn't love her husband anymore and now she wants a new life. Her new path leads her into the arms of another man, because her destiny is to have two more children with her new partner. Her husband is very upset that his wife has left him and is incredibly jealous that she has found new love, so he casts a spell to win her back. The spell works and the ex-wife becomes confused. She experiences loving feelings for her ex-husband again, so she leaves her lovely new partner and returns to the unhappy marriage. Her future children are unborn and she has not progressed in her spiritual development. She is now rehashing old lessons and is stuck.

It could get even worse! Let us say that it was the husband's fate to meet someone new—a wonderful lady who would help him and take him in a new direction. Because the spirit world plans everything in our lives, he meets her anyway—after having dragged his wife back to him, now the husband falls madly in love with his spiritually intended partner and leaves his wife for her. The wife still has the powerful spell influencing her, so she falls to pieces and is unable to move on with her life. Sound far-fetched? Well, it isn't. I am asked repeatedly to undo such spells, and frankly, they are not easy to reverse. Incidentally, the husband will incur a great deal of bad karma for his actions, and at some stage in his life, he will learn some very hard lessons!

The point I am trying to make is that *you must never cast a spell to win back someone you have lost or to make a particular person fall in love with you.* This type of personal gain isn't spiritually ethical, and it can cause a great deal of harm.

So now you may ask, is it safe to cast a spell to bring romance into your life? The simple answer is yes, it is safe, as long as you don't have any specific person in mind. For example, if you are simply lonely and hoping to meet someone nice, it's fine to cast a spell for romance, but if you want to draw the attention of someone specific—and *especially* if he or she is already partnered with someone else—you will bring nothing but trouble to yourself and to everyone else involved.

When a Lover Leaves

This spell will help a person come to terms with losing his or her partner.

On a Friday evening, run yourself a warm bath. Add three drops of lavender oil, two drops of rosemary oil, and a handful of salt. Light a white candle and relax into the water. Meditate on the one you have lost for about five minutes and imagine your ex-partner being in a happy situation without you. However upset or angry you feel, it is imperative that you try to make your thoughts as positive as you can when thinking about your ex-partner. This gives the spell the power to work.

Next, imagine that you are holding a large crystal ball, and concentrate for about five minutes on sending all of your unhappiness into the ball. With your eyes closed, envision throwing the ball out to the universe. Breathe steadily for an additional few minutes.

After you have finished bathing, place the lighted white candle beside your bed for fifteen minutes. From then on, each time you start to feel unhappy, light the candle for half an hour and then blow it out.

Move on and Overcome Bitterness

Amazingly, making bread is famous for diffusing pent-up emotions. In ancient times, if a person was angry, he or she would make bread in order to focus the negative energies on something other than the problem. By punching and kneading the dough, you will rid yourself of any inner frustration. Once the dough is in the oven, the smell of the fresh bread cooking will give you a feel-good factor, healing the mind and soul. This spell works by combining magical ingredients, which will change your frame of mind and sweeten your mood. As an alternative, you can perform the spell while making gingerbread.

Find a good bread recipe that appeals to you and follow the instructions. When you knead the dough, say this incantation repeatedly, until you have completed the process of kneading:

My anger will die
In a blink of an eye.
With this bread
Heal my heart and my head.

When the bread is cooking, sit by the oven and inhale the aroma. Once the bread has cooled, spread a hearty slab with real butter and concentrate on the soothing taste. This will be quite a powerful loaf, so be sure not to let anyone else eat it.

Coping When a Marriage Breaks Down

The breakdown of matrimony is undoubtedly stressful and often traumatic. Whether you are relieved that your marriage is over or devastated that it has come to an end, this spell will help you to cope with the ordeal and will result in newfound confidence.

In the evening, place three tall red candles—representing the past, the present, and the future—on a table. Next put three level teaspoons of allspice in one small bowl, place three bay leaves in another, and fill a third small bowl with pink carnation petals. The bowls don't have to be a matching set; any three small bowls will do. Place one of these bowls in front of each of the three candles. Light the candles and say the following incantation nine times:

Shianna, angel of love,
I summon thee to give me strength to move forward from this marriage.
Let my spirit have the confidence to go forward without regret.

When you have recited this nine times, close the spell by saying "So mote it be." Then allow the candles to burn for two hours before blowing them out.

Place the allspice, bay leaves, and petals in a small drawstring bag, and pop them inside your pillowcase for the next nine nights. For each of the nights, let the three red candles burn for half an hour. Within a week, you will be feeling much more self-assured and focused.

The Death of a Loved One

It might be hard for us to understand, but sometimes the spirit world separates us from the one we love. Everyone knows that some people deal with grief differently than others. There is no set time frame given to the grieving process, and sadly, some people never get over losing the one they love. We can perform spells to lessen the pain and to assist us in coming to terms with our loss. This procedure goes hand in hand with understanding why we have to be left alone, and allows us to identify with reincarnation and the learning process of life.

1. Begin on a Friday.
2. Choose a pink candle.
3. With a small knife, inscribe the candle with your name and the words "To ease the loss of love." Place the candle in a holder and light it in a quiet room of the house. Recite the following incantation seven times:

   Archangel Metatron,
   Help my soul to heal from the separation I have just incurred.
   Melt the pain like the wax of this flame.
   Bring peace into my heart and spirit.
   And let me love again with no regrets.

5. After you have recited the spell seven times, say:

   And so mote it be.

6. Repeat this spell for the next five days.

Attract Romance with a Love Pouch

Any ritual that takes time and energy to create has far more effect than a spell that can be done quickly. Love pouches really do work, and people have often found a nice partner by making one. The magic begins when the person actively starts to assemble the pouch. Each item either is found by the spell caster or is personal to him or her.

While making the pouch, project your thoughts toward the kind of person you wish to meet. This process adds to the potency of the spell, which in turn directs itself back to you.

You will need the following:

- A white handkerchief
- A needle
- A small piece of paper
- A pink ribbon
- Two or three personal items
- Some lavender oil

Place the needle and the personal items into the handkerchief. On the piece of paper, write your name and the words "To find romance" and place it inside the handkerchief. Gather the corners of the handkerchief together and tie them with the ribbon; then perfume your bundle with some lavender oil. Lay the pouch on a table and light a small pink candle.

Say the following three times:

Blessings bestow,
For love will grow.
My heart is free;
Bring joy to me.

Leave the pouch where it is until the candle burns down; then put the pouch in your bag or somewhere on your person every time you go out.

A Quick Spell to Find Love

Begin on a Friday.

With a sharp knife or pin inscribe your name on a pink candle (a small tea-light candle is fine) along with the words "To attract love."

In a quiet room in your house, place the candle in a holder and light it. Wrap a length of red ribbon around your left hand three times. Face your candle and recite the following three times:

Be rid of my solitude,
No more alone.
Soul to soul,
This is my goal.

After you have recited the spell three times, say thank you to the angels and sit beside the candle until it burns out.

Invite New Love into Your Life

Add the petals from two red roses to your bath water. Take a bath; then, before you empty the tub, collect some of the water and a few of the petals and place them in a small bowl. Light two red tea-light candles and say:

Passion is mine
And all is divine,
To be worshiped and loved
Together entwined.

When the candles have burned down, scatter the water and petals outside. Your new love should cross your path within a few months.

CHAPTER TWELVE

Spells for Health, Wealth, and Prosperity

Before we reincarnate on Earth, we speak with our spiritual advisers, who make us aware of every lesson that we will be learning in our lifetime. Through hardships, we develop and move higher up the sacred ladder. The basic life issues we all confront relate to our security and well-being, and when life issues are compromised, we are stressed—we need to learn to find resolution and peace through these hardships so we can move on in our spiritual development. The life areas of most concern are our health, our wealth (whatever you understand that to be), and how we prosper in life.

Health

Undergoing certain health issues contributes to our growth and progress, so it isn't always possible to cast a spell to heal illness. For years, I have performed rituals to help cure my autistic son, yet nothing I tried seemed to work. My very wise mamma explained to me that we cannot change certain things and must not try to. My son has taught the family so much, and as a result of this, we now possess a great deal of knowledge on autistic spectrum disorders. This knowledge has enabled me to help other parents going through similar circumstances. If my son had not been born with autism, I would not have started a support group in my area, and teachers, specialists, and other people who have helped him would have been deprived of this experience.

It is quite rare to cure a terminal illness successfully with the use of magic. This is because illnesses are often karmic and arranged by our guides and helpers before we reincarnate. We all agree to take on some pain and suffering, and every child that is born causes the mother pain during labor, so the process starts immediately. In my many years of spell casting, I have known of only two occasions when the individual has been cured of a terminal illness. These instances occurred when the sufferer, or the person who cared for the sufferer, summoned the angel of healing, Raphael. Angels can create miracles if they have authorization from the higher realms, so it is worth giving it a try. Direct communication with the angel and a series of prayers are needed. This process may take days or weeks, depending on whether the angels are allowed to intervene.

On a more realistic note, one can make a spell to alleviate the *symptoms* of illness and also to ease minor complaints. The spell below will help to ease any form of pain and suffering.

An All-Purpose Health Spell

Place a gold candle (you can use a yellow or orange candle as a substitute if you don't have a gold one) in a holder and situate it in the center of your altar before lighting it. Sprinkle a handful of sea salt around the base of the candle holder, encircling it. Place a photograph of the sick person on the altar and chant these words nine times:

Magical power is here this hour;
Illness is gone; there shall be none.

Wealth and Prosperity

Never feel guilty about conducting a spell to boost your cash flow. Money is a form of energy, just like everything else. When funds are limited, we can spend so much time worrying that we lose sight of more important matters. Before you begin a spell for money, it is important to realize that your spell will not work unless your need is genuine. If your aim is to win the lottery simply because you want a lot of money, it is doubtful that your spell will succeed. Greed isn't tolerated by the spirit world. You are far more likely to get just the amount of cash that you need.

I once cast a spell to win a jackpot of nine million dollars, and the same evening I won ninety dollars! Not really needing any extra funds, I planned to spend the cash on a few luxuries. Unfortunately, the very next day, a filling dropped out of my tooth, and the dentist bill was eighty-five dollars. I gave the extra five

dollars to charity and thanked my guides. If you do receive magical money, you must always give a small portion of it back to an aid organization or to someone who is desperate. This keeps the good fortune circulating.

The Wish Board

A very good way of attracting the things you need is to write them down. About a year ago, I was given a fancy blackboard to put in my kitchen. It was similar to the type that you would write your shopping list on. Being the kind of witch that I am, I had to experiment with it, and as Christmas was just around the corner, I decided to cast a spell for a bit of extra cash.

With some white chalk, I wrote on the board "Leanna will soon have extra funds, so mote it be." I drew a little pentagram on the board and left it to see what would transpire.

Three days later, my husband was opening his mail, when he nearly fell over in surprise. There in front of him was a check from the Internal Revenue Service for more than a thousand dollars. He had apparently paid too much tax and was being refunded the difference. He looked at me and I looked at the wish board. A coincidence? Maybe—or maybe not!

Since then, I have tried the technique many times with different wishes, and most have been granted. Any kind of blackboard will do; for instance, the one that your children have in their toy box. If you cannot find a blackboard, a large sheet of paper will work just as well.

Money Spell 1

Finely chop about ten basil leaves and place them in a bowl. Light some frankincense, and once it has burned out, collect the ashes and mix them with the basil leaves. While you are stirring the two together, say repeatedly, "Wealth is great; this is my fate." Scatter the mixture outside your front door to attract money to you.

Money Spell 2

Put seven coins in a clean glass jar. Screw the lid on tight and place it on a high shelf in your home. Shake the jar every day and say, "Money for me, so mote it be."

Money Spell 3

On a Wednesday morning, draw a pentagram on a piece of paper and place five green candles (in holders) on the five points of the star. Position some coins in front of the candles and put your checkbook nearby if you have one. Light all five candles and recite the following invocation:

Let the flames burn bright:
Money in sight,
Luck will grow
With this I know.
So mote it be.

Let the candles burn all the way down until they are extinguished. If you blow out the candles, this spell will not work.

CHAPTER THIRTEEN

Spells for a Happy Family

It is quite safe to cast spells for children if they are going through problems or difficulties. Because children have lived on the Earth plane for only a short time, they are closer to the spirit world than adults are. This often makes them more psychic and open to receiving magic.

To Conceive a Child

Cut a small circle out of a stiff piece of white card stock. You can also use a flat pebble as an alternative. With a red pen, draw two circles on the card or pebble, one inside the other. Charge the magical amulet by saying:

Spiritual forces,
This symbol I show,
For within my body
A child shall grow.

Carry the amulet with you all the time and place it under the mattress when you make love.

The Badly Behaved Child

I am a great believer that extreme behavior in children is usually the result of some kind of underlying problem. This spell will get to the bottom of the problem and reveal to you what is causing your child to be badly behaved.

On the evening of a new Moon, place something that belongs to your child, such as a baby bangle or a favorite toy, on a flat surface and surround it with some small amethyst crystals. Silently ask

Paige, the angel of children, to help the child stay calm. Say this prayer three times:

With all of my power
I ask for your help.
Bring forth the reasons
Why my child is aggressive.
Surround her with your light of wonderment
And bring harmony into her heart.

When you have repeated this incantation three times, put the item back where you found it, and put the crystals under the child's bed.

To Give a Child Confidence

I always like to use magical dream pillows with my children to combat any particular difficulties they may have. To boost your child's self-esteem, sew together two squares of white cotton on three sides. The size of the cloth bag isn't important. Inside the bag place some rosemary blossoms and three small sprigs of heather. Write your child's name and the word "confidence" on a piece of white paper and add the paper to the contents of the bag. Finally, sew up the opening and place the bag under your child's pillow.

Families at War

Sibling rivalry is common in families, and heart-breaking though it is, there is rarely anything you can do to resolve the situation. Some believe that we reincarnate with the same circle of people from previous lives and that conflicts over trivial issues could be the result of a dispute that has been carried over to this life.

To unite your children, a harmony spell is required. Take a photograph of each of your children and glue the photos together with the pictures facing each other. With a yard of white silk thread, bind the photos around and around, saying this incantation repeatedly until the thread is fully wound:

Blessings bestowed, you will no longer fight;
With harmony strong you shall unite.

In ancient times, the mother of warring children would take a lock of hair from each child's head and braid them tightly together.

Family Luck Spell 1

If your family is experiencing a run of bad luck, try these powerful positive spells to change your fortunes from bad to good.

On the first night of a new Moon, take twelve white candles to the kitchen (the heart of the home) and place them in a circle on a table. Inside the circle, place a picture or an ornament of a white unicorn. The unicorn symbolizes the purest of all creatures, and it will bring a change of luck and an abundance of love into the lives of its keeper. Light the candles and say the following words three times:

Take forth this ill luck
And bring peace to its space.
Magnificent Moon,
Engulf and embrace.
Angel of harmony,

Shine magical power.
All that is harmful, be gone in this hour.
So mote it be.

After one hour, blow out the candles. Repeat this process for the next three nights.

Family Luck Spell 2

We often go through periods in life when we are tested. Negativity breeds negativity, so it's important to clear out the psychic debris and change the energy around you to a positive one.

This can be done in a number of ways, but a good method is to start by having a really good spring cleaning in your home. Get into all the nooks and crannies, clearing away dust and cobwebs.

Place plants such as ferns and geraniums all around the house. These plants have protective properties, so they will banish any bad luck that has attached itself to your home and family.

In the evening, light three white tea-light candles in every room of the house. Go into each room, throw a handful of salt on the floor, and say this spell:

Ill fate be gone;
I shall have none.

This spell can be done whenever life is becoming tedious. You should notice changes for the better almost immediately.

Become a Better Parent

Whether you need to instill more discipline or to relax your attitude, become more sensitive, or simply muster the strength to cope, this spell will help you to gain wisdom and clarity.

Place two mirrors and one white candle on your altar. Position the mirrors so that the flame is reflected in both mirrors. Sit quietly for a few minutes concentrating on the candle and then say:

Gusto and strength,
Sit firm in my soul.
Peace and serenity,
This is my goal.
Trouble-free times
Bring effort with ease.
Increase my vigor.
I ask this, please.

After about an hour, blow out the candle. Repeat the spell again each night until you feel more confident.

CHAPTER FOURTEEN

Spells for Career and Willpower

Ultimately the career path you choose and your success at your job are dependent on your hard work, your talents, and your commitment. The same can be said of the hard work you do to improve yourself, whether that improvement is weight loss or smoking cessation—your inner drive and commitment are what fuel your willpower. However, every now and then, in every struggle and time of hard work, adding a little extra magic to the process doesn't hurt!

Career and Work

New Job Spell 1

Whether you are desperate to find a job or are just seeking a change of career, place the following ingredients into a saucepan:

2 teaspoons dried basil leaves
2 teaspoons allspice
2 teaspoons cinnamon
1 bay leaf
Peel of 1 apple

Add to the pan 1 cup of bottled spring water. Bring the potion to a boil. Remove from heat and allow to cool. Drain the liquid through a sieve, discarding the apple peel and bay leaf, and pour it into a screw-top bottle. Finally, add 6 drops of bergamot oil and a few drops of green food coloring. Shake the bottle every day for a month, and a new job will follow.

New Job Spell 2

This spell will work only if you have had an interview and are awaiting the results. Write yourself a letter or send yourself a congratulations card like this:

> *Dear [your name],*
> *I would like to offer you a job within my company.*
> *Congratulations!*
> *The Boss*

Be sure to write the name of the company somewhere on the letter, and then mail it to yourself. You will be sending out a positive message that symbolically works with constructive projection. This spell can also be used for any exam situation or a driving test.

Improve a Failing Business

Go to your place of business and scatter citrine oil in the four farthest points of the building. This will remove any blocks that are preventing your business from being successful. Hang lucky heather in the window before leaving.

Willpower

Addictions—Smoking, Alcohol, and Drugs

Spell casting to stop addictions requires a great deal of focus, but this can be achieved by making contact with the subconscious mind. It may take several months for a spell of this kind to work, so you need to remain determined and patient.

The spell below can work for a drug or smoking addiction, as well as over-dependence on alcohol.

Find a small pebble or flat stone, from either your garden or the beach. Cleanse the stone in salt water and dry it with a cloth. With a permanent marking pen or paint, write the word "stop" on the stone.

Arrange a further twelve stones of similar size from your garden in a circle on the ground. On the night of a full Moon, place your amulet stone in the center, along with a piece of kyanite crystal. This precious crystal will increase willpower. Leave the stones overnight to absorb the Moon's energies, and by the morning your amulet will be fully charged.

Keep your magic pebble and crystal on your person at all times and your cravings will fade away.

Weight Loss

Chamomile is one of the safest and gentlest of all the herbs. It relaxes the senses and magically cleanses the system. You can buy tea bags from your local supermarket, or infuse one tablespoon of the fresh leaves in a teapot. Leave them to brew for a few minutes and then pour the tea through a strainer into a cup. Drink the hot liquid, and with each swallow, close your eyes and imagine yourself being your ideal weight.

When you have finished the tea, sit quietly and say these words:

I cleanse my soul to reach my goal.
The power of will I shall instill.
Healthy within, slender and slim.
So mote it be.

You can repeat this spell whenever your willpower is failing, or simply perform it every day so that you remain in the right frame of mind.

Some Final Thoughts

This book is meant to be a plain and simple introduction to Wicca. The contents of this book just scratch the surface. It shows you the first steps to developing your potential and achieving your goals. Before you begin to really understand the "wise arts," you must follow the gentle rules discussed herein, and spend some time thinking about what it means to follow the Wiccan path.

On many occasions I have been asked, "Why did you become a witch?" or "How do you know you are a witch?" The answer to both is that anyone can call herself a witch and simply decide to follow the Wiccan way of life. After all, the word "witch" is just a name, in the same way that "Christian" or "Buddhist" is. The heart that you put into your path is what matters; not the name.

I discovered magic quite by accident. I was twenty-one years old, married, and suddenly facing adult life head-on, out there in the big wide world. Everything was a struggle; life was no longer the carefree existence I had as a child. I got to a point that I suppose was the only time in my life that I had really knelt down, clasped my hands together tightly, and prayed. I lit a pure white candle and prayed to the angels. I asked for courage and money. You name it, I asked for it—over and over again. After what seemed like a few hours, I woke up from the sleep into which I must have fallen. The candle had burned down, and so I took my tear-stained face to bed. The next day, my stepfather called to ask me how I was doing. Not wanting to reveal my financial worries to him, I lied and said I was all right. Well, I guess he must have known me better than I thought he did, because later that day he called me back and said, "How much money do you need?" The tears flowed again as I poured out my predicament. That afternoon, I had another call from him to say that he had transferred the funds I needed into my bank, and from that day on, I didn't look back. I have since asked him how he knew what to ask, but he had no answer to give me. I can only suppose that the angels had a quiet word in his ear when he was asleep!

I started to read as many books as I could find on magic and to teach myself about the Wiccan way of life. I encourage you to do the same.

Good luck, and may the angels bless you all.

Acknowledgments

To my ever-supportive stepfather, John Greenaway, who has read through this book very carefully and did so several times. Without his dedication and commitment, I'm sure these pages would not be as magical as they are.

A big thank-you to my dear friend Sasha Fenton who has encouraged me to write and helped me to fulfill a lifelong ambition.

To Beleta Greenaway. I picked her brain to the limit in order to make every spell a success. Her love and guidance are always present, and whichever path I have chosen to take in life, I can always hear her footsteps right behind me. Thank you, Mamma.

Latest Releases in the Plain & Simple Series

Numerology
Anne Christie

Healing Herbs
Marlene Houghton

Meditate
Lynne Lauren

Astrology
Cass and Janie Jackson

Chakras
Sasha Fenton

Crystals
Cass and Janie Jackson

Fairy Lore
Ralph Harvey

Palmistry
Sasha Fenton

Runes
Kim Farnell

Tarot
Leanna Greenaway

Totem Animals
Celia Gunn

Other Titles in the Plain & Simple Series

Angels Plain & Simple
Beleta Greenaway

Body Reading Plain & Simple
Sasha Fenton

Chinese Astrology Plain & Simple
Jonathan Dee

Color Therapy Plain & Simple
Nina Ashby

Face Reading Plain & Simple
Jonathan Dee

Feng Shui Plain & Simple
Sarah Bartlett

Flower Essences Plain & Simple
Linda Perry

Handwriting Analysis Plain & Simple
Eve Bingham

I Ching Plain & Simple
Kim Farnell

Medicine Wheel Plain & Simple
Deborah Durbin

Psychic Ability Plain & Simple
Ann Caulfield

Reflexology Plain & Simple
Sonia Jones

Reiki Plain & Simple
Philip Jones

Reincarnation Plain & Simple
Jass and Krys Godly

Sun Signs Plain & Simple
Sasha Fenton and Jonathan Dee

To Our Readers

Hampton Roads Publishing, an imprint of Red Wheel/ Weiser, publishes inspirational books from a variety of spiritual traditions and philosophical perspectives for "the evolving human spirit."

Our readers are our most important resource, and we appreciate your input, suggestions, and ideas about what you would like to see published.

Visit our website at *www.redwheelweiser.com*, where you can learn about our upcoming books and also find links to sign up for our newsletter and exclusive offers.

You can also contact us at *info@rwwbooks.com* or at

Red Wheel/Weiser, LLC
65 Parker Street, Suite 7
Newburyport, MA 01950